"Reading this book gave me a look inside my life. I am not an adoptee and was born into a white Christian home; however, I could relate to many chapters of this book. As I was reading, I placed myself into character and questioned my intentions. Did I show enough of a caring and concerned attitude toward others, in specific situations they may encounter that I may never understand thoroughly? Did I help or hinder in the process of them trying to find themselves? I want to be a positive influence in all situations. This book has made me search for ways I can make a positive impact on those around me."

—W. B.

"This book provides an amazing insight and perspective into one women's personal journey with adoption, discrimination and infertility. V. Lakshmi openly shares her thoughts and feelings about what she endured with honesty and courage. Her detailed analysis of her emotional and thought-provoking experiences provides the reader with great insight, empowerment, hope and encouragement. This book is not only an outpouring of a truth that is generally not acknowledged within today's society, but it is also a cornerstone of perspective for all of us to build upon."

—H. R., LCSW

"V. Lakshmi bravely converses with the reader in her heartfelt spirit of perseverance, acceptance and love! This memoir is a testament not just for women, but all humanity, in facing head on the fragilities of life's nuances, coming to terms and making a difference!"

—D.

"A refreshing glimpse into the psyche of someone searching for their identity and the trauma inherent in this pursuit. A must read for anyone contemplating adoption, with the added perspectives including dealing with the loss of motherhood due to painful endometriosis, and the dilemma of always feeling different as an Indian brought up in a white Jewish family. Many questions arise when meeting new people. Lakshmi describes dealing with a fair amount of discrimination. The question 'where did I come from?' must arise. Fortunately, she has a loving, supportive family. I suspect her journey in India has just begun."

—L. R.

FINDING YOUR WAY

When Life Changes Your Plans

*A Memoir of Adoption,
Loss of Motherhood and
Rediscovering Home*

FINDING YOUR WAY

When Life Changes Your Plans

*A Memoir of Adoption,
Loss of Motherhood and
Rediscovering Home*

V. Lakshmi

Library of Congress Cataloging-in-Publication Data
Lakshmi, V.
Finding Your Way When Life Changes Your Plans:
A Memoir of Adoption, Loss of Motherhood and Rediscovering Home
p. cm.
Paperback ISBN: 978-1-947708-07-5 • Ebook ISBN: 978-1-947708-10-5
Library of Congress Control Number: 2018966163
First Edition, December 2018

ⒸCITRINE PUBLISHING
Asheville, NC, USA • (828) 585-7030 • www.CitrinePublishing.com

To my husband:

There are no words to describe fully how much I love you and appreciate you. Thank you for always encouraging me and for believing in me. You have helped me to reach for the stars, even in times I didn't think I could. I'll love you forever.

To my family:

It was written in the stars for us to be together. Your unconditional love and support is profoundly appreciated. I am who I am because of all the life lessons you have taught me. I consider myself blessed to have you as my role models. To my niece and nephews, I strive to be the best role model for you and I will be there for you always and forever. My heart is filled with the love I have for the four of you. I love you all.

To my friends:

Thank you for all the laughter, support and longs talks over lunch or coffee. I treasure each of you. Thank you for lifting me up when I needed it most.

Table of Contents

Preface

Modern life hinges on an elusive idea suggesting that our life is laid out for us. That our path is supposed to be what we had always envisioned it to be. That any dream we hold dear is supposed to come to fruition. That all the wishes we ever had as children should come true, and that life is set up the way we want it to be. But we face a huge reality check when life has a different plan for us, when our rainbow and cotton candy dreams are destroyed and we are forced down another path, searching for a new light to guide us on our way.

Do we crumble when are dreams are taken away from us and the universe decides to guide us in another direction? This is an experience I have encountered too many times in my life. Imagine being on a cloud floating… and then the cloud drops you to the ground, over and over. Where is the next cloud that you step on to carry you up? Do you create the next cloud, or do you let go of your dreams and take your chances by stepping onto one of the next clouds to appear? Who controls your destiny? You or others?

My life has been guided by a series of events that have shaped and defined me—from overseas, cross-cultural adoption as an infant, to growing up an Indian Jew in the suburbs of America, to my own infertility and adoption challenges and an eventual hysterectomy that has led me to redefine womanhood not on any culture's terms, but my own. I always heard from people that I should write a book. My story is not common, and I am sharing it in hope that you see that no life vision is set in stone and there are many ways to re-write your life. Yes, it is exhausting to keep recreating yourself, but through the *light* we can all reach, float upon the clouds, and realize our destiny in the stars.

Since the purpose underlying this book is tied to my life story, here is a short biography, just for a backstory. This book is not about me. It is about giving you and anyone else who reads it inspiration to pick yourself up again and continue to find true joy and love. My goal in this world is to help as many people as I can. I will not leave this planet without reaching that goal. It sounds cliché, but I do believe we all can make a difference in this world by sharing our stories.

Where do I begin? Many people believe that my life was written in the stars, that my destiny was written before I even had a part in it. With this I fully agree.

Why?

Too many things occurred without my doing or control over my life. All of these events helped shape me into who I am today. This is a person who is forever changing, and molding and also trying to find the true me... I am still searching to find out who I am as I am sure that you are also. My own *self-identity* is what I have struggled with my whole life.

I was born in Tamil Nadu India in 1976. My birth mother died two days after giving birth to me and this has thus far been a lifelong struggle for me. As every birthday rolls around, as birthdays do, I face the guilt of my birth mother's death. The guiltiness eats away at me. How does one let go of it? My birth father tried to take care of me for five months but since he was unable to provide milk, I was given to a woman who was building an orphanage. I lived in Dr. Pauline King's home while Family Village Farm was being built. It was with this woman, who has saved hundreds of children's lives, that I remained until I found my forever family, a kindred clan from the United States who adopted me in 1977.

I have been and remain utterly blessed to be part of my forever family. None of what I say about identity is about them. It is my own feelings and my own personal journey. They have supported me every step of the journey from the day we met until this very day.

I am an Indian woman adopted by a white Jewish family, and this is only part of *who I am*. Early on, this was a deep struggle for me. Adoption wasn't quite as commonplace in the '70s, and there weren't as many mixed families as there are now. I didn't quite fit in. I fit in with my family, but not anywhere else.

I attended a Jewish private school, where I fit in because I was Jewish after all. Then I went to public middle school and public high school, where I struggled to fit in. I despised the middle and upper school years and couldn't wait to attend college, which proved a longer-than-usual journey once I completed my degree in 2017. Today I have a Bachelors of General Studies with minors in Psychology and Gender Studies.

In my studies, I observed the ways identity is influenced through the religions and nations with which we identify—and where those intersect with our passions. My religion was chosen for me because my parents were Jewish. Although I love the religion, I am not religious. I love the culture and values of Judaism. Like most children, I didn't have a say in my religion; it is what I was adopted into and yet being Jewish is something that I am proud of. I also identify as a United States citizen with a profound love of country. Its ideals inspire me to give of my time and talents through volunteer work as a freelance photographer, as I have done for eight years as of this writing.

Photography is my love and passion, and it helps me to express myself. Through living out the dramas I describe in this book, photography is how I finally came to identify myself as an artist. It is clear as day to me that I am not happy unless there is art in my life, whether it is in the form of a painting, photography, writing, or dancing. Above all, photography has been and always will be something that helps me to lift myself on the cloud again, when I didn't think I could climb again, from a devastating loss. Photography saved my soul and brought me back to life.

My wonderful cousin and I sat by the ocean one day. We were talking after I'd suffered a deep loss, and he sensed I was trying to find my way. He asked me, "What do you love to do? What makes you happy?"

My reply came effortlessly. "Photography," I said.

"Then why aren't you doing what makes you happy?" he asked.

Within weeks of this discussion, I started my photography business. I thank him from the bottom of my heart.

Through this decision, my role and goal in this life has evolved into the one I mentioned at the start of this chapter: *to help as many people as I can before I die.* I volunteer as much as I can and will always help people. That love of charity comes from my parents and extended family. Charity is something that I have always witnessed. Deep inside there are other reasons why I love to help people, including how I love to see them smile and laugh. To me laughter and joy is something that there is never enough of, ever.

I have seen a lot of sad terrible things in this world due to my travels and work. Yet, through the sadness, I see there is a joy in the darkness. I have met some of the most grateful people in this world *who have nothing* and are in the worst situations possible, but are so happy with what they have. These people who I have met have really taught me life-changing lessons I will share in later chapters.

In my life, I have done many things to pay the bills, as we all have. Way back when, they may have seemed like J.O.B.s yet all of these roles have shaped my identity. I have been a waitress and an assistant manager and I have trained restaurant employees for a franchise across the nation (which ties into my love of food... something I don't hold inside, as you will see). I was also a teacher for many years. The more years I live on this earth, the more I see how each role we're assigned plays its perfect part.

A teacher is originally what I wanted to be as a child. Teaching is a path I was sure that I would be on forever, but life went another direction—or so it seems. I am one of those people who always wanted to try many different occupations. Early in my career, I earned a Child Development Associates degree and worked as a Pre-K and Kindergarten teacher. Children remain a huge gift to me, as I have learned a lot from them. Everything I discovered as teacher has helped me in my studies in Psychology, which in many ways the children I taught inspired me to pursue. When I hear people say that they are just doing what they were trained to do, or that they feel stuck on a plateau in their careers, I feel bad for them because I wonder if they realize that they actually do have a choice.

My job is not what defines me and never will. It is *who I am as a human being,* and what I do with people on this earth, that defines me. The moments I am helping family or a friend are the ones that shape me. And then there are those intimate moments spent with the love of my life (my husband), who is my best friend; I truly believe the stars were lined up for us to meet. We don't have kids, but we have a dog who is our baby and together we are a family. (More on my love of dogs and animals and my passion for helping them, coming up.)

In a word, through this short synopsis I aim to have provided essential background information for you to not only understand me but also find your own connection to my story as you venture forth into these pages. A vast assortment of reflections about gender, race, religion, nationality, adoption, health challenges and the state of modern medicine—all tied to this foundational exploration of identity—will piece together as the book unfolds. It is my deepest wish that you find friendship and understanding in this story of how I found (and am still finding) my way when life reveals its own plans, time and time again. Above all, may you find inspiration to live a beautiful life, no matter how the winds of life direct your course.

CHAPTER 1

Who Am I? Free-Floating in Questions of Identity

Identity is a word that has been following me around for more than forty years. *Who am I? Where do I fit in? With whom do I belong?* I have struggled to fit in my whole life, lacking clear answers to these questions. Most of my life has seemed like a free-floating, out-of-body experience. The moments when I feel whole are usually when I am with my husband and my immediate family, and now with the beautiful community of people reading this book. It's the other moments when I wander outside of myself and look for a place to land that I truly feel as if I am free-floating.

Growing up, I fit in my family but nowhere else. Not in school, not even at my temple, not anywhere. It's hard to be a Jewish Indian woman in America. Try to imagine for a second that you are Indian and Jewish and living anywhere in the United States. That's not to say that my adoption by a white Jewish family wasn't meant to be. Lined-up stars has been a theme in my life and I do believe it was destiny to have gotten the exact parents I have. They both found out about me on the same day from two different people. They already had two biological children together and wanted to adopt their last child. And later in life, the stars lined up again for me to find my husband, a co-worker of one of my brothers. I am unconditionally loved and accepted by all of them. I do believe that it was destiny for me to end up a part of this specific family, and that all things happen for a reason.

That doesn't make being a minority in America any easier. It remains a constant struggle for me. I have faced too much racism and discrimination in my life, and yet I still choose to rise above the hate and remember that the people who spew vile words and actions my way are dealing with their own issues, not mine. I believe in *karma* and treat people the way I wish to be treated. I don't have a racist bone in my body, and wish people would see me for who I am and not for my religion and the color of my skin.

The first time I returned to India in 2013, I had the wonderful experience of being in a majority for the first time in my life. Wow! What an eye-opener! What a glorious experience! Swimming in a sea of faces that looked like mine. I wasn't alone and it felt miraculous—and still feels this way when spending time with my close Indian girlfriends.

If you have never been a minority, try putting yourself in one's shoes once. You might learn a lot, and will almost certainly cultivate new depths of compassion for people. Fitting in is something every human being wants; feeling loved, not judged, is what most people strive for. To fully love someone, you have to love them unconditionally, and not be judgmental.

Can you count on your hand how many people you can truly be yourself with?

I come from two different worlds and countries that I love with all my being. I love America, and I love India. I consider them both my homes. I was adopted from India, the land of my ancestral ties. America is where I grew up, and it is my country too. People who have two homes, or connections to another country, can relate to their heart being split in different locations, the land from where you come and the one where you grew up in. India and America are both my identities. It is possible to love two countries and call both of them home.

Still, I hadn't returned to India until 2013, when I was in my late thirties. I wish I had studied my cultural roots while I was growing up. Anyone who is adopted from another nation should go back and study where they come from, if they can. It truly helped me to find a missing piece to a puzzle that I had been trying to solve my whole life. I also have a family that supports me in searching out my roots. I am lucky that way. I have friends who are adopted and they are so concerned about their parents' feelings, and about hurting them, that they will not return to their birthright country or search their roots. Yet it is so important to do that. We are all born in a certain country, and that we had no control over. And this country holds clues, if not the keys, to our heart.

By now it's no secret that I was one of the lucky adoptees. I got a great family. I am close with my parents. I treasure them both. The adoption identity struggle I know in my bones has nothing to do with them—it always was a struggle to find people who look like me. Struggling to fit in is common for adopted children.

Along the way, too many people have offered unsolicited comments about "how I was saved by my family" and that "I should be grateful for very opportunity that my family has given me." Believe me, I *am* grateful for that. Yet I have also often wondered why I should feel like I owe my life to them when in reality I had no say in being adopted.

I love my family and believe I was meant to have them, but did they really save me? When people ask what I am doing to "return the favor," I often wonder if this same expectation is also placed on biological children?

My own parents would agree that the best way I can "return the favor" is to shower love on the children in the orphanage from where I came from, to love and support these children as I was loved and supported by my parents. Often I do just this by fundraising and offering my other gifts, like photography. I don't help out of guilt, I do it because I love these people and I want to support them in any way that I can. They fill my heart and soul, and I will help them till the day that I die. They are my Indian family. Trust me when I say, they have taught me more than I will ever teach them. They have filled a huge hole in my heart that no one else can fill. And unless you have been adopted, please have a sense of compassion and understanding when you are speaking with someone who has been adopted.

Here are some of the issues of adoption that have plagued me my whole life:

- *abandonment issues*

- *separation anxiety*

- *trust issues*

- *need of acceptance*

- *fear of rejection*

- *being able to fully connect with someone*

Throughout my life, I have been told that, even though I am a die-hard friend, I am not able to open up and to share with them as much as they would like me to. That has come up a lot for me. Multiple people have said they wish I would share more. I am learning to do that. I have often wondered whether it is possible for an adoptee to completely transcend the fear of rejection at the core? I would love to hear other adopted people's views on this and if they have the capability to truly share from their soul? Can adopted people truly be an open book? Is transparency meant for us?

I come from a strong family where everyone has a powerful voice and the capacity for transparency. So I questioned, due to the lack of biological connection to them, if their strength to speak their truths was inherited. Perhaps this was something I just didn't get from my ancestors. Inside, I reflected: *Is our core personality genetic or culturally conditioned?* The *nature versus nurture* debate has always fascinated me. Why? Because as an adopted person, I was left no keys to my biological family.

Am I the way I am from my genetics, or is it because of my upbringing? It's a common question of the adoptee's heart. I have spoken with adopted people who have met their birth parents after decades of separation, and they are shocked and amazed at how similar they are to them! They share talents and personality quirks. There is often a striking resemblance for them in the way they act. It makes sense, especially when you look at biological parents and their children. I know an adoptive father who said that when he met his son's birth mother, it made sense the way his son was. He too questioned the *nature versus nurture* debate, just from a different angle.

Imagine for a second, never seeing someone who looked anything like you. Or wondering where you got your nose or eyes from. Or longing to know whether you share the same smile and personality traits with anybody else? These are common questions that I hear from adopted people. Aren't we entitled to know that?

I don't share traits with my family at all. The only thing we have in common is that we all have big hearts and would help anyone, something taught to us by our loving parents.

Despite sharing this most important thing, I always felt different from them. They are all highly intelligent people who are highly successful at what they do. Even though I got my strong work ethic from them, I always felt inferior. This was not of their doing, but a result of my own insecurities.

I congratulate my family on all their successes—I am so proud of them. Yet I wish people would not have compared them to me, like the school teachers who assumed I'd be as school-smart as my brothers because we had the same parents. Why did they not have the sensitivity to consider the role of my genetics? Their comparisons only fueled my insecurity. I am sure all of you out there reading this have experienced the sense of inferiority once or twice in your lifetime, too. It is a human dilemma, after all.

Going back to school after almost a decade, I finished my college degree in 2017. Whether you call it nature or nurture, finishing my degree was crucial for me. As an aunt to three nephews and a niece, I wanted to be a role model to them. Even though the day after graduation, I was in a three-way discussion with my best friend (who is also different from her family) and my mother. I was asking my mother, *How could I compete with our family's successes and intelligence?*

I almost had an out-of-body experience when I shared this with her because, as my mom sat there listening, I realized that it might shock her to learn that I felt this way. My mom is one of my best friends and I am always and forever wanting to protect her feelings (which she does not need at all, but it doesn't stop me from trying). As I spoke from my heart, she was able to hear this for the first time. She helped me realize the many levels on which I do contribute to the family. It was a crucial thing for me to hear... because deep down, I had wondered, *did I ever contribute to the family?*

I doubted my inherent worth because negative messages had taken over. When I took Cognitive Psychology, a fellow student once asked, "How come we hold on to the negative comments that people say? Why do they ruminate in our heads?"

The professor explained that *it takes ten compliments to erase one negative comment.* Wow! That was interesting to learn. But how sad is that?

My identity used to be defined by negative comments that tore me up inside. I've been called too many racist words due to my skin color and religion. Based on nothing more than a glance it's been asked of me, "Are you sure you can afford to shop in this establishment?" and "What, are you stupid?" Some who have known me as an acquaintance have dared to comment on my weight and the fact that "she's not providing children to her husband." As hard as I've been working to let it all go, I would be lying if I said derogatory comments about my religion, the color of my skin, my intellect, and my female body didn't bother me. No one is made up of a hard steel plate that protects us all the time.

My wish for the world is that will we be kind to one another and speak from love and, not hate. I still feel those certain words that were spoken decades ago like daggers through my skin. Sometimes they still cause me to put on an armor of emotionally defense myself the minute I walk out of the front door. Many people say, "Don't let people words, have that much power on you." Yet that's easier said than done.

Words have consequences. People's hearts are sensitive. Consider that person you are speaking with may be soul-searching to reconcile questions of their identity. May we all think before we speak.

CHAPTER 2

Endometriosis, a Failed Adoption and the Loss of Motherhood

For as long as I can remember, I wanted to be a mother. It was part of my life's plan. I had dreamt about it when I was little, admiring my mother and aunt as role models. My mom should win some kind of an award, as she is still mothering us in our forties and fifties—she is truly the definition of a mom who does not quit. Never do I remember her not being there for me. She'll hop on the plane the instant she knows I need her. How can I tell her that she is the sun, moon and stars to me? I hope she knows that.

When I talk about stars being lined up in my life, my mom was meant to be my mom. That I don't question. The fact that she's my adoptive mother doesn't change my love for her, or my biological mom, or the mom who cared for me until I was adopted. My mother who has had me since I was about eleven months old first explained to me that love is love when I was having a really emotional time, trying to digest everything that I'd learned about my biological roots during my recent time in India. In fact, I have been blessed to have three mothers all within a short time span of eleven months!

I treasure my mothers for their beautiful impacts on my life. Is it any wonder I wanted to be a mom too? Never would I have imagined that I wouldn't be a mother. I love kids. They rock! I adore their sense of wonderment, curiosity and pure innocence.

I also love their questions... so cute! Recently, a child asked me, "Is there food in heaven?" I told him I would do my best to find the answer. Anyone out there reading this, please let me know if you know the answer to this question. Would love to get back to this child. I know too much about the pain of unanswered questions.

Why Endometriosis and Why Me?

In 1997, I got really sick with severe menstrual issues. At this point in my career, I was a teacher's assistant at the time living in one of the southern states. I had to take a lot of time off, due to the pain, which could be immobilizing for me. I'd had terrible periods my whole life—I know many women out there can relate. But in my early twenties, it got severe. I went with my mother from doctor to doctor seeking a diagnosis or some explanation for the pain. I sought the counsel of every doctor imaginable, even an orthopedist. I subjected my body to multiple tests, from a bone scan to multiple MRIs and ultrasounds. Unfortunately, no one could help me.

Eventually, I would have to go to the ER for pain. It was there that my parents and I came across the most arrogant and obnoxious doctor. I was lying in the bed, writhing in pain when he said to my parents that there was nothing physically wrong with me, so there must be something psychologically wrong with me. Well, he didn't know my mama and papa bear! They weren't having it... how dare he say that in front of me. He was another person, who spoke before he knew. (I eventually got an apology from this doctor, who personally called to express his regret over the misdiagnosis.)

Luckily, a parent of one of my students recommended a different doctor. By the end of the first consultation, he was one-hundred percent sure I had endometriosis. Endometriosis is when the lining of the uterus detaches and grows in other parts of the body. Back in 1997, doctors didn't know a lot about it, or at least the doctors I'd come across. The doctor I met with was well educated on endometriosis.

He diagnosed me with Stage 4 endometriosis and sent me into the first of many surgeries for my endometriosis. This amazing doctor saved me and I am forever grateful to him. He was a pivotal person in my life. He affirmed me and treated my case with profound attention to every detail. When I said that something was wrong, he listened and believed me. Not only did he treat me like a human being, but he respected me and understood that I was more than just a number. I wish more doctors would listen the way he did. Since this time, I have been misdiagnosed three more times for other health issues.

I am not one of those people who believes that doctors are gods and that we should believe everything that they say. They are human beings who make mistakes too. I have learned this over the years, yet too many people put their doctors on a pedestal and will not question them at all. In general, why aren't people questioning them? Too many doctors have made mistakes with me, so I am sure that my view is a little jaded. Yet once in a while we find the rare gems who go above and beyond for their patients—and when we do, we should shout their names from the rooftops.

Healing from endometriosis has been a twenty-year journey, but it doesn't have to take that long! I feel and pray for all the women who suffer from it. I believe I got it from my birth mother because it is considered to be a genetic disorder with a polygenic/multifactorial inheritance, which means some inherited genes from my mother may have contributed to the disease. You have to look to see whether the traits were influenced by the environment. Where is the placement of the genes? Endometriosis might be the reason why my mother died two days after giving birth to me. Again, I will never know the answer to that question, which I have to accept along with not even knowing her name.

In my head, I tell myself this story that she had endometriosis. Again, I am an adopted person who is trying to piece together my past with little to no information. What could be the reason for my endometriosis? Try for one second to imagine what it would be like to have no medical history? It is extremely hard to find peace, not to mention fill out medical forms, a major frustration of adopted people with whom I have spoken.

The dream of being a mom has been like a cloud and bubble burst right in front of my eyes, multiple times. I am sharing my heart and soul here, because I know there are other women out there suffering from this disease. I know they share a common thread with me.

Let's fast forward, a bit. When I got married to the man of my dreams. We were ready to start a family. We tried the natural way and were unsuccessful. We worked with a specialist and tried hormones and a slew of other treatments. For the women and couples out there who are dealing with infertility issues, my heart bleeds for you. Because it is a painstaking process, an emotional roller coaster of too many ups and downs.

The hormones pumped into your body don't help you either! Eventually we were told that it wouldn't be possible for us to have children. We had tried multiple methods that failed. Soon we found ourselves in the process of moving to another state, getting adjusted to our new surroundings, and working at new jobs. Then magically, after feeling a little weird and missing a period, we decided to take a pregnancy test and... wow, we had done it on our own. We were pregnant! I can't begin to tell you the joy we felt. We floated up on the cloud that carries your dreams and holds them tight for you. We had arrived on that path of our dreams!

Then one cold rainy spring night, after a glorious day of playing with our nephew at a museum and being with family, I felt weird. When I went to the bathroom, the blood I saw terrified me and we rushed to the ER.

You know the thing they do, where you get an ultrasound and the tech won't talk to you until the radiologist reads your chart? We sat there and looked at the screen and we were beyond overjoyed! How silly and stupid I feel now.

Then we encountered another heartless doctor who came in and told us point-blank, "Your baby has passed," then turned and walked away from us. Really.

"Are you fucking kidding me, is compassion *not* taught at medical schools?" I said as the door closed behind him. I don't know his name, but I can still see his face.

Luckily we had the most amazing nurse in the world, who sat and cried with us. Let's hear it for the nurses in America, they really are the backbone of the health care system!

It's strange, I can't tell you what I did or ate five days ago, but I remember everything about that day. It was a long time ago. Apparently it's called an episodic memory.

I remember the smell and the sound the rain, blending with the comforting embrace of my gentle sister-in-law, who was with us at the time. She held me as I cried, as a little child cries. I remember calling our families to tell them. That's a hard call to make. My family was on the plane shortly after to be there.

There was another reason why this loss was *beyond* devastating for me and my husband. It is a horrible loss for anyone and I don't wish it for anyone. And I felt another loss, besides the baby dying—it was going to be for me the first time I would have had a known biological connection to someone. I'd yearned for that my whole life. I was going to see a person with my nose and eyes and all the parts of me and my husband combined. That was a profound loss, too.

I was so naïve to think that it couldn't happen to us. I walked around when I was pregnant seeing those butterflies and cotton candy dreams. Was I arrogantly to think we had done the inconceivable to have gotten pregnant without the doctor's help? We had beaten the odds and *no one* was going to ruin the rainbow I was walking on. Life had changed my plans again.

Jewish people have a certain way to handle death, and it is very precise and it creates a mourning period (Shiva). The family surrounds the one who is grieving and takes care of them during the mourning period. I was used to that, watching grandparents die and other family members. But I didn't understand the grief process of losing a baby. There would be no Shiva. No ceremony, no funeral. When exactly is the mourning period for losing a baby? How on earth do you mourn?

The whole thing is downright depressing. There isn't an answer. I didn't realize until later, when the grief kept coming up, how I needed some kind of ceremony.

The next morning after the miscarriage, I woke up to the murmur of voices in the kitchen downstairs and debated whether putting my feet on the floor and going downstairs would make a difference, in contrast to my main thought: *screw it, I'm staying in bed.*

I'd arrived at one of those of those crossroads moments: should I curl up in a ball and disappear in the covers, or lift myself up?

To this day I don't know how, but I lifted myself up.

The cloud that I had been naïvely riding the day before was gone, and my soul had suffered a hard fall to the ground. SMACK!! But I needed to know how my husband was doing. People forget that husbands mourn a miscarriage as much as women do. I have seen some of the toughest men I know, when they have lost a baby through a miscarriage, cry just as hard as their wives. My husband was dealing with his initial grief and loss, but being the gentleman that he is, his first concern was *how was I and what could he do to help me?* My concern was *how was he,* so I lifted myself up out of the bed to find him and reassure him that *we are a team and we will work through this together.* That is when my sister-in-law suggested that we go buy a tree and plant it in the backyard.

We did it that day. My husband, brother-in-law and sister-in-law planted a really beautiful tree. It is still standing today. I like watching it come to life in the springtime with its pretty pink flowers, and how it changes colors in the fall. This ceremony helped us tremendously. I have shared the idea with other couples who have suffered this loss and it seems to help. Please pass this on to people you know who have miscarried; it will make a difference in their grief process.

The other ceremony that has helped us is the angel ornaments that we put on our Christmas tree every year. (My husband being Christian, we celebrate Christmas, and me being Jewish we also celebrate Hanukkah.) We have passed that on to friends too. I have bought several an angel for their tree.

People always say there is a lesson, and it's wrapped up in my least favorite saying, "God has a plan for you." I know they mean well, but unless you have been through it, there are no words to describe the pain of the loss that is miscarriage. Notwithstanding, I appreciate the outpouring of love and support my husband and I received as we otherwise dealt it in our own private way.

I didn't get the lesson of the miscarriage till later on, when I started helping friends going through the same process, girlfriend who just needed a friend who had been through it. In those conversations, which led to writing about my experience for others to feel my heart when I say, "I see you, I understand," I have found my own higher purpose.

When a woman's dream of birthing a child is destroyed, she wonders, *how am I going to find my way forward? What is my new path? Where do I start again?*

At this point in my journey, it looked like my endometriosis was back and I would require yet another surgery. Once again, I went under the knife to get everything cleared out through a laparoscopic surgery. That was supposed to help me get pregnant again. Yet, this time, I had a wonderful doctor who gave us no guarantees. We tried another assisted procedure to increase our odds, and it failed too.

When we went back to the doctor, he spoke with us about continuing procedures or investing the money in adoption. Since the fertility treatments were expensive, he suggested it might be another route we would want to explore. So adoption would be the next step on our path into parenthood.

Jump to years later. There was a year I like to call *the year from hell.* Haven't we all had a year like that? A year we wish we could just wipe away from our memories. Just wave a magician's wand and make it go away from our history.

So we passed the home study, the thorough process that

future parents undertake when they are seeking to adopt. It includes background checks, home inspections, and many reference letters as well other legal documentation. We had the baby shower and we built a beautiful nursery through the help of our families. Which in retrospect, we wish we hadn't. There is a Jewish custom where you wait till a baby is home, to build a nursery in case of a sad situation. But I'd been adopted and how could an adoption possibly turn out to be sad?

We didn't have a nursery to come home to after the miscarriage and I truly wish we hadn't for the adoption either. But we were *so ready* to get ready to be *hopefully* picked as parents for adoption.

Then I broke my leg and ankle, by slipping on ice. That was emergency surgery, meaning pins and plates in my leg and ankle, and a long nine months of physical therapy. Which we would mean that we would have to wait to start the adoption process, again.

At last, we were ready. Gorgeous nursery with all our dreams encompassed in that single room. We stuck out the waiting period for adopted parents, waiting to get picked. It's hard, because we just sat and waited for a phone to ring. It is nerve-wracking, knowing that the birthmothers have seen your information and they have studied you while we, on the other end, have no information on the birth mother.

The system (in the United States, at least through my own experience) is set up for the birthmothers and not the potential adoptive parents. Granted, my opinion is highly jaded because of my terrible experience. While I am living my truth with this book, I am owning my faults as well. I have processed a deep well of resentment and hard feelings when it comes to adoption—and through it I have learned firsthand that you can't judge people for the feelings that they have. Our feelings are our own and not to be judged.

I have heard stories of great adoptions in the USA. That was just not our situation. I will not name the agency we worked with, because there are potential adoptive parents out there who are still on that magic cloud, and I hope all their adoption is smooth and wonderful. Yet I will share, for the sake of potential parents out there trying to adopt, some of the lessons we learned so that our unfortunate pitfalls may be avoided. In no way, am I an expert in adoption, but I hope my experience will help people too.

So back to the cloud, which took us a couple of years to be elevated too through hard work. Having reassembled shattered dreams of a baby once more, I could see the positive in every situation again. I could even see the halo of pink around my clouds.

So, we got the call. When you get the call, you are picked! You have twenty-four hours to get on the plane, get there, and meet your baby. Let me try to explain the emotions at this moment: joy, excitement, nervousness, happiness on a level I had never experienced (except the day I married my husband). A lot of rushing around and packing, interspersed with calls to the family that we were chosen. Pretty much a frenzy of emotions, as you can imagine. But we had imagined this dream into being and we were to meet our daughter the next day. We had a wonderful name picked out for her.

Was I naïve? We were picked by a woman on the East Coast. I thought it was *meant to be* because, even though we reside in the Midwest, I'd grown up on the East Coast. What are the chances? In a short while, I would be hopping on a plane back to the very state where I had grown up. I foolishly thought the stars were magically lined up, down to the location. Foolish me. But boy, were we ready.

Off to the airport, we hugged our dogs and told them in the squeakiest voices we were bringing them a sister. We barreled into the airport looking like parents, stroller and all the baby gear that you would ever need. We were *prepared* for her. People were smiling and a few even looked at the empty stroller and asked, "Are you adopting a baby?" We smiled and said, "Yes!"

I remember that flight. I travel a lot and can't tell you every flight I have been on in my life, but I remember that one. Back to the East Coast!! Where it seemed things were circular and coming to full enclosure. I have a big heart for the East Coast. I love everything about it. Yeah, so not only was I on a cloud, but I was among the clouds on this flight, grinning with joy and excitement! I should state that sleep hadn't been a priority with us getting ready. We were flying on adrenaline.

When we landed, we were instructed to go right to the hospital to meet her. We did as we were told. Let me state that the agency had no one there to meet us or work with us; all communication had been through the phone. In 20/20 hindsight, I see it: *What the hell?* Please be cautious of that if you are adopting. What exactly is the agency supplying you? Who will meet you there at the hospital when you get the call? These are some questions you'll want to ask. Our agency did everything through the phone and through email, and we didn't know to ask these questions.

We come from families of successful people and friends who are gifted and talented. We had a lawyer and a social worker, both available to us via phone, and they were a lifeline. We couldn't have made it through those twenty-four hours without them!

In stumbling around during the adoption process with blinders on, I could not see the red flags about the agency I worked with. Because I had wanted to have a baby so bad, in my eyes they were my allies! They could do no wrong and how naïve I was to think that.

Any person or couple wishing to adopt should open their eyes with adoption agencies and be aware of the deep-pocket factor. Because adoptions cost a lot of money, and money was the least of my concerns the months leading up to the day we went to meet our daughter.

Once we arrived at the hospital, we were told we'd meet the birthmother before meeting the baby. We did as instructed and we met the wonderful woman who was about to give us her baby. We sat with her and cried with her and thanked her from the bottom of our hearts. I felt compassion for her and yet I was still jumping up and down inside with joy and excitement. Then we were told we could go meet the baby. It had arrived, the moment we had waited many years for, the moment were about to become parents of a newborn baby daughter.

We entered the secure nursery area and there she was. Talk about instant love and connection. The moment of becoming a mom and dad was finally here!!!

You don't know my husband but he's a teddy bear and a love muffin. There is not an unkind bone in his body. I love him more and more every day, and I don't take that for granted. But there was something about seeing him holding her that melted my heart in a way that was an indescribable feeling. I thought, as this baby was in her future father's arms, how lucky she was. Because my husband was going to be an incredible father. And how lucky we were that this baby was going to be ours.

We sat there and held her for quite some time. We took photos and floated on the cloud so high in the sky, there was no way we would come down. Right? Wishful thinking again. How in the world could we possibly fall again after losing a biological child? There seems to be no way that something so heartbreaking could happen to us again. A harsh reality check was coming and it wasn't going to be easy.

Then we got a call that we needed more papers notarized. Because adoptions are all about the paperwork, crossing t's and dotting i's. So we had to leave and find a notary downtown in a major city, under a time crunch. I don't know why we didn't ask the hospital for a notary but we didn't. So we went downstairs to tell the birthmother we were wrapping up the paperwork.

Please know we were deeply respectful of her and kept our emotions under control when we were with her. We acknowledged what she was going through. When we left her room, we looked each other.

"Something's changed," I said.

Nodding my husband finished my thought when he said, "There is something different in her eyes."

We brushed it off, left the hospital and made our way to town to complete the paperwork. We returned to our hotel room to set up the crib. We now had been awake for more than twenty-four hours, but adrenaline carried us through the busy city. There seemed to be a floating movement to our footsteps, almost like dancing a waltz.

Have you been so happy that you floated and skipped, and the happiness inside you was a visceral response? *Delight. Gaiety. Elation. Bliss. Pure ecstasy of happiness.*

Did all those feelings stop and change drastically? Yes. Allow me to explain. Things unraveled quickly, and we lost the baby girl that we fell in love with. The birthmother ended up keeping her, which she was fully entitled to do so. There is even more to this story, but I am choosing to not go there again because it is too painful to express in words. You might not even believe if I told you all of it. Sometimes, in my head, I still don't believe what happened.

In a nutshell, we were strongly advised by our social worker friend and family lawyer, whom I trusted with my life and still do to this day, that we should strongly think about the situation. The agency working for the mother did not have our best interests at heart. I strongly advise anyone who is going to adopt to find out if both biological parents have relinquished their parental rights. That is something that I wish we had known about.

There is a ten-day waiting period where a birthmother can change her mind, and we had known that. We had accepted that. But at this point, I was no longer functioning. I remember being in our hotel room in tears, and my husband had to physically lift me up to put me in bed.

My husband grabbed the phone from my hands and told the agency that he would be the one speaking and dealing with them. Which was deeply appreciated, because I could barely speak or breathe.

The next day, we found out the baby was taken home with her birth mother. I believe now that it was this girl's journey to be with her mom. I wish them nothing but peace and love. We found this out a month after we returned to the agency to have a serious meeting.

We didn't get back on the plane, instead driving the whole way home, staying with family along the way. There was no way in hell that I was going to push an empty stroller through the airport again. Just the imagery of it was too much for me to handle. Empty stroller. It's weird, years later I still feel almost paralyzed by that image.

I remember my husband getting the crib out of the hotel room, as fast as he could for me. The hotel staff went above and beyond for us, and I'll be forever grateful to them. They were incredible human beings who saw what happened to us and really were decent and compassionate. I still remember the woman's face at the front desk. Her heart was real and genuine, and so appreciated.

That night we were going to get sleep, get up and hit the road as early as possible. Happiness had been replaced with despondency, and a deep, empty, emotional, gnawing- numbing sensation had taken over, the same one I'd experienced when we miscarried. I resisted the emotions as they came back, after I had worked so hard to overcome them. It seemed to be like a really bad déjà vu. WTF? *Why?*

It transmuted to emotional numbness where I almost didn't feel anything at all. It was like walking around in a state of haze and I believed I would never see through that haze. The pain was literally eating me up from the inside. I didn't even know pain could do that. Did you?

Outside a literal fog hung around us and I barely remember the ride home. I do remember parts, because we had a lot of family support and calls on the way home to reassure us that we weren't alone. I stared outside the window as we traveled home along the East Coast, passing so many sites heavy with memories. My husband had never seen where I had grown up, so I wanted to share with him my childhood home. I knew in my heart, there was no way in hell I would be returning to this state anytime soon. So we took a trip to my childhood neighborhood.

So we did that and it took my mind off the pain, a little. One more thing that helped the next day was returning to a favorite restaurant that our family had gone to a lot. For anyone who is a foodie and grew up on the East Coast, we have this passion for good food. I am a foodie and love food, and it provided the source of comfort that I needed that day.

An Italian meal never tasted so good in my life. Yes, I'm a Jewish woman from India but Italian is my favorite food.

And returning to this childhood restaurant somehow saved my life that day. Looking back, I am sure it was a way to feel my family close to me. I would love to share the name of this special restaurant and tell the owners and staff how they helped me, yet I am aiming to preserve a certain level of privacy in this book. But oh how they revived me that day, it was *the perfect* place to be!

I smelled the familiar, wonderful Italian spices, flying through the air. The smells of pizza, lasagna and garlic filled my soul and I felt at home nestled there in their booths. We sat and ate and I think my husband ate too, finding solace in the food. I could hear Frank Sinatra in the background. His voice had never been so soothing and the combination of the post-meal endorphins and Frank Sinatra's songs practically lulled me to sleep.

On the way home, it was like being stuck in a state of trauma where the shock of what just happened, hadn't quite registered yet. The sight of the stunning mountains didn't even affect me. I am a nature girl and they had no impact on me at all.

Nature usually heals my soul, but I was angry at the world, and this was an anger that I was not accustomed to. I never believed in carrying anger with me; I understood what it could do to the body and overall health. Somehow I wanted to feel well enough to take all the hurt away from my husband. When you have a love like we have, there is a symbiotic connection, where you feel each other's pain. I wanted to wave that magic wand, which we all know does not exist. Would someone please create it?

What in hell had just happened? There was no rational thinking going on; it all had gone out the window with our dream. I was not sure exactly what was taking over, my body or my mind, but either way, all the way home I was contemplating whether or not I could lift myself up again. *How many times could I do that?* And this was not a sea of not "poor me" emotions, but an honest river of questioning. *Did I have enough resilience to do this again?*

Have you ever been so tired that your whole body feels depleted from all the emotions? Like you could feel the exhaustion wallowing in your cells. I was already emotionally exhausted from the miscarriage . . . could I forge forward?

Into our driveway we pulled and my husband, being the amazing person that he is, ran inside, dashed upstairs and shut the door to the nursery. I came inside and hugged my dogs (we had two at the time, one has passed since that time). We had rescued them both, and they were our babies.

What I told my dogs in that moment was: *no one will ever take you away from me.* I held them and they sensed my sadness and one of them curled up in my lap. They didn't really leave my side for a couple of days, sensing I needed the extra love. Dogs are amazing! They know you better than you know yourself and make the best therapists.

The first couple of days home were a blur. I barely moved off the couch and the bed, eating all my comfort foods. Funny how food can fill your soul, and lift you even if it is just for a little while.

When you are a highly sensitive person, there are pros and cons. Making decisions through one's heart, and thinking after—that can be a pro and a con. The highly sensitive are also the target of insensitive people, although not quite sure why that works that way? The raw nerve I was, I should probably not have picked up the phone that week. We had full family love and support, and yet some of the advice I received was just plain thoughtless. Unfortunately, I was too depleted to reply then, but it's helped me create a dynamite list of what not to say to a person who has just lost their dream of parenthood:

- **"Just get over it."** Granted, this came from someone who had not been through what we had just been through.

- **"I don't have time to have lunch with you, I'm too tired."** Really are you kidding me?

- **"I will not listen to you cry."** Wow. So then you will listen to me scream? The sheer meanness of the words just infuriated me.

- **"You should've given your husband children."** A complete stranger said that.

I needed help processing everything—and I realized it. So I saw a therapist at the recommendation of my doctor. The diagnosis was PTSD and anxiety. It was explained to me that it was way too many emotions for a person to go through in a twenty-four-hour period. I know from studying psychology how important and helpful talk therapy can be. I do not believe a person is weak because they see a therapist. Actually, I think it shows strength and humility when you realize you need help and actually ask for it.

The therapist helped me go through everything, and she taught me a lot. Knowing how much I loved my dogs, she encouraged me to walk them in the morning, as the exercise would nourish my system with good endorphins. She also advised me not to open the nursery door for one month. She also recommended that I avoided all baby sections in stores, for a long time, which made complete sense to me. It was good advice.

After a month, we opened the nursery, packed up everything and donated it all to a women's shelter. The furniture we donated to very good friends of ours whom we love. They were about to have a baby girl. We love that little girl and we are so happy that she has it. You might wonder why I would share of all of this with you and the world at large. I am sharing it because there are other couples out there who have gone through the same process, and could feel alone—and if you know someone who has been through infertility or adoption, or meet someone who is going through it, or find or have found yourself in a similar situation, you'll know—without a doubt in your heart—that even in a world graffitied with signs of cruelty and insensitivity, *there are people who understand.* And there is still hope for a beautiful outcome of endometriosis.

To this day, when we meet people, they often ask, "Do you have kids?" We say no and offer no explanations. We don't share our story with anyone, unless we truly know them. Writing this book may change that, but until then I take solace in the caring people of this world. They are my family.

Many months after the adoption crisis, my husband and I began to re-entertained the thought of having a traditional family. And that's when the most obvious thing finally hit me: *We are a family!* And we will never let anyone take that away from us.

Women are defined by a couple titles or roles that we play. There is being a girlfriend, a fiancée, or a wife. There is the title of being a mom.

I lost my identity when I lost the dream of being a mom. I'd thought in order to be a woman, you had to be a mom. It took me years, to realize that *I am not less of a woman because I am not a mother.* I have many girlfriends who are not mothers, due to either medical reasons or by choice, and they are all living full healthy lives. I never thought of them as less than a woman, so why did I conceive of myself this way?

I also thought adoption was meant for me, especially because I was adopted. I have come to understand that the universe has other plans for me. As I have given up the notion of planning everything, I now watch the universe guiding me in the direction of places that I need to be.

With all those grand plans for motherhood I had since I was five years old suddenly put to rest, I would have to find my new plan. It marked the beginning of my finding my new path. Or allowing the path to be recreated for me, and letting things unfold naturally.

What would happen to all of us, if we stopped planning every excruciating detail of our lives and we *just started living* our lives? Are people capable of that?

I don't even know if I could stop planning. I'm a big planner! In fact, in writing this book I do have a plan. I dream of kindling within people a belief that, no matter what hardships they are facing, they can recover and see the light again, even if all they see right now is darkness.

CHAPTER 3

Hysterectomy: Losing My Uterus, Finding My Womanhood

Flash ahead to 2015 and 2016. Over a twenty-year span, I'd had several more operations for endometriosis due to further complications. Whenever I start to add up the number of operations, plus at least two knee surgeries and leg and ankle surgery, I give up. I have been under the knife more times than I can count. I also seriously question the amount of anesthesia that has been injected into my body and what the long term effects of it will be (not sure if I truly want to know the answer to that) but I am grateful that I have woken up every time.

So it came to pass, due to an endometriosis situation too painful for me to write about, that it was time to have a partial hysterectomy. Today I only have one ovary left. My doctor felt I was too young to not at least keep one, as I was just entering my forties when this occurred.

What an emotional process! What a painful process! And the worst recovery ever! Friends who had been through it warned me about the recovery, but OMG, the after-pain was utterly horrible, not to mention debilitating.

Talk about recreating a path in life after losing a sense of "womanhood." The hysterectomy was a success in that I no longer suffer from endometriosis, but medical professionals *need to help prepare women for the emotional aftermath.*

Doctors are so clinical that many seem to forget there is an emotional being inhabiting the body that they are treating.

Fortunately, my doctor was excellent. I had done about three surgeries with her, so I felt secure. I just wish I had learned more beforehand about the emotionality of it. There are still days when I am trying to figure out if I am less of woman because I no longer have a uterus. I don't know yet, but I do feel *way* better not dealing with physical pain anymore.

Isn't that a strange thought, though? To think I am less of a woman . . . is that even possible? I'm still me. One man jested with me after the surgery, "Do you feel like you weigh less?" His lighthearted spirit made me smile, and laugh, which is exactly what I needed then.

It took patience to retrain my brain that I am still who I am with one less organ—that I didn't lose the core of me. As I was told by a highly intelligent woman, "It is like a part of you is gone physically, but you do retain all the femininity you have always had." A year later, I fully agree with her. I celebrate that I am no longer in pain due to endometriosis. It's a disease that keeps rearing its ugly head... and the women out there who suffer with it know exactly what I am talking about. And our sisters who don't know this pain, you are blessed.

All of my infertility issues were traced to endometriosis, so I am happy at least knowing that the cause of the suffering is no longer. Throughout my twenties and thirties, I lived with a haunting feeling that my female organs were failing me. For two decades I searched for answers, desperate for some resolution. It seems like the hysterectomy has done that for me.

But to truly reap the healing benefits of the hysterectomy, deeply emotional work had to be done. For one, *I had to let go of the anger of my body failing me.* I had to realize that I am the same feminine woman I have always been. It's not like when people look at me, they know what's not there. And in a way, I have enjoyed the freedom of no period anymore! I have a couple girlfriends who envy this about me, especially when they are struggling through "the monthly beast," as my girlfriend jokingly calls it.

And so the partial hysterectomy proved another moment where my life course was altered. Was it the answer to the end of my endometriosis? Only time will tell if the condition is truly gone forever from my body. Yet the hysterectomy symbolized a door that was finally closed. Through that closed door, I learned once again that, although we might have the best of intentions and lay out our life neatly in our notebooks or iPads, it doesn't mean it will unfold as we have imagined.

When the winds of life blow me off my cloud, I don't know if I am resilient or just conditioned to keep picking myself up and getting back on it. Is it a survival mechanism within me? That when the cloud falls, I find myself grounded again on this Earth and I have to replant my feet. Haven't we all recreated ourselves time and time again? Maybe, I have wondered, are we better off for it?

CHAPTER 4

Grief, Loss and the Way Forward

Grief is something we all face in our lives. Whether it was the loss of a pet, a family member, a divorce, the loss of a child, or anyone else we have lost, grief comes in waves. It often rears up when we least expect it, forcing us to deal with it. For decades on end, I pushed grief way down hoping it would just disappear.

As a lifelong student of psychology, I am a big fan of Elisabeth Kübler-Ross's work on grief. Here is one of my favorite quotes from her work:

> "The most beautiful people I've known are those who have known trials, have known struggles, have known loss, and have found their way out of the depths."
>
> —Dr. Elisabeth Kübler-Ross
> *Death: The Final Stage of Growth, 1975*

Somehow this quote connected with me. Maybe it is her general understanding and praise of people. If there would be a report card for grief, I would have gotten a big fat F, the reason being I have not fully dealt with it. I don't know why... maybe because it is too painful to deal with?

Somehow in my head, I've likened it to opening Pandora's Box and feared I wouldn't be able to close that box again. I have felt angry at the grief!! *Why, should humans continue to suffer over and over again?*, I once wondered. Then I got the answer from a cherished mentor, R.G.: "If you don't deal with it, it will keep coming back."

Has anyone else been angry at their grief? Is it justifiable in my thinking, that there should be an end to grief? Or does grief have its own schedule?

I still wonder about these things.

Painting, writing, photography and walking are all activities that helped me process grief, and they are still helping me. In no way am I an expert in grief; I am just someone who has experienced way too much of it in my life. I understand that what works for one human being facing grief is not going to work for another human being. Yet I have felt inspired to share some tips that were passed onto me.

I had a therapist who knew me to be an artistic person going through grief. She suggested that I start painting again. In no way am I a Picasso, or Michelangelo, but what I painted came flowing out of me. It definitely helped and for a while I painted for fun, because I found it deeply relaxing. Eventually I took an oil painting class and came across another professor who said "to give up" and that "I would never be a painter." She was so unaware of how those words influenced me. After, I didn't paint for ten years.

Even with everything negative I have seen and witnessed, I still am a woman who sees the glass as half full. I am naïve, some say, but I say the world has enough grief and why add to the weight of it?

By no means have I mastered grief. I don't know if I ever will. In my case, I have wondered, *how does anyone ever get over losing children, whether biological or adopted? How does a woman who wants to be a mother grieve the loss of the chance of having a child?*

I have spoken with a wonderful psychologist about this. I was not seeing him as a patient, but as a friend. He told me after the miscarriage, "You are not just mourning the loss of the baby, but the first biological connection to someone." It made profound sense to me.

It also made me wonder if other adopted children who face infertility issues come across the same issue. *Does the lack of biological connection for adopted men and women who can't have children affect the adopted grown woman and man in a different way?*

Infertility hurts and affects all women and men, whether they're adopted or not, and is something that I don't wish upon anyone.

Earlier I wrote about the tree we planted in our backyard after the loss of our biological child, per the suggestion of my sister-in-law. It helped tremendously with our grieving process, along with another tip passed on to me. A wise friend suggested that we create our own ceremony.

She said, "If there is no ceremony for miscarriages, then

make your own." So we released some rose petals into a body of water and watched them float away. No words could explain the healing effects of following this truly great advice. I don't know what it is about water, but there's something peaceful and cleansing to the soul to sit by the ocean or a lake and listen and watch the rivers flow. I pray that this bit of advice that was passed on to me ripples out to help another person who has miscarried and is looking for a way to heal from the grief.

My friends who have miscarried have expressed and reflected my same confusion about the fact that that there is no funeral or grieving ceremony for miscarriages. *If we don't create a ceremony for miscarriages, is the grief process somehow halted? Or has society at large wrongly assumed the natural process of grief is not going to occur?* I would love to know the answers to those questions.

Does Grief Have a Higher Purpose?

Over the years, I have tried desperately to figure out why I have faced so much grief in my life. The only conclusion that I have come to is that it has helped me support friends going through the same process. Where they were at a loss for words on how to move forward, I was able to pass on wisdom learned from those I deeply trust. *There may never be an answer in this world, why we go through half the shit we go through. Maybe no answer is necessary.*

To be clear, I do not advocate not a "poor me" mentality. It's the inquisitive side that interests me. I want to understand the fundamental reason for all the sad things that happens in this world and why so many people suffer from grief? We've all heard that *"what breaks you down, makes you stronger."* Yet I am not a fan of such clichés. People reiterate them way too often and they have all lost their meaning to me.

When looking closely at the words, one has to wonder: *Is grief breaking you down to build you up? I have not gotten to the good parts of grief yet. Are there any good parts to grief? Why is that we have to be torn down first to our emotional core when we lose someone we love? This is why the funeral for is for the living and not the dead.*

I've always wondered, when the funeral and ceremonies are over, when someone we love has passed, and the family is no longer surrounding the grieving person, *is that when the silent grief begins? When we are simply there, alone with our thoughts? In the middle of the night, when we are lying in the bed, staring at ceiling, thinking of whom we lost—if the ceremonies worked, then why does it come so strong then?*

Grief is one of the emotions that lingers, at least in my personal experience.

I just don't know if there is a set rules of how we are supposed to feel after someone we love dies? I certainly found no rules on dealing with the loss of a child, which I would never wish on anyone. I truly carry the families in my heart who have been through it. It's so sad and it stays with you. Prayers and peace for those families.

I think it's beautiful in this world, how every culture honors grief in a different way. Every religion has its way of dealing with grief. It seems like there are a lot of people in the world trying to figure it out. On that note, there has to be a better way to train doctors who are telling people they miscarried, and better protocols of communication between the intake and outtake staff. Literally I felt I was in the "care" of the coldest doctor in the world. Then, as my husband and I were leaving the hospital, a nurse who did not check our chart said, "Hope everything goes well with the baby!" in a cheerful annoying voice that I wasn't ready to hear or receive. I did not respond in a nice way, which is not my typical behavior. I said something that I am sure shocked her. In the end, all I meant was, *really, you didn't check our chart?!*

All of this I have shared not to complain but with the prayer that perhaps the nuances of my personal story may inspire awareness, sensitivity, and compassion in often unexplored areas of the human heart.

Is It Goodbye Forever?

To say goodbye forever... it seems too long till we see each other gain.

So we won't say goodbye, we will say *we will meet when it is meant to be.*

Why we were separated?

Why didn't we ever meet?

I look up to the stars thinking, *you can see or feel us,* but can you?

Did you hear and feel our salty tears at night while we cried in our pillows?

Are you there watching over us? Will we ever meet again?

Did we ever fully connect? Did you hear the prayers we had for your future?

Did you feel that unconditional love we were going to give you?

Did you hear me singing to my belly while you were there, even if just for eleven weeks?

Did you carry the love we had for you all the way up to heaven?

Are you alone? Or did you find

the ones we have lost before you
and did they greet and hold your
hand till I get there...

Did you find Zaddy?

Do you know that we still carry
all of you in our hearts and souls
and that you are never forgotten?

Do you feel the sun in your face
and the ocean waves crashing on
your toes?

Do you dance and twirl? Does
your laughter fill the heavens? Do
the stars light your way?

For the eleven weeks we had you,
you were ours and we loved you.

We thank you for the time that
you spent with us... our little
Angel.

The joy and love you gave us is
irreplaceable and we will hold you
again one day.

V. Lakshmi

CHAPTER 5

The Waves Beyond Grief: PTSD and Anxiety

I had come home from the East Coast emotionally spent. Needing to find my way again, I sought therapy and was met with a diagnosis of post-traumatic stress disorder (PTSD) and anxiety. To this day, I offer only my opinions about the meaning and impact of these diagnoses. I am not in the medical field, nor am I dispensing any medical advice, just sharing my experiences with this dual diagnosis.

Where do I begin? I'm sure that everyone reading this is somehow connected to someone that has PTSD or knows someone who has anxiety. Both of these diagnoses can shape and change a life. It doesn't mean that getting these diagnoses define who someone is as a human being. In my opinion, these labels don't make one less of a human, who has to be handled as a fragile piece of glass.

It baffles me that some people don't believe in PTSD. My guess is that they are probably the same people who have not been diagnosed with PTSD. Has anyone ever been though a life-altering trauma and out unscathed? I know many people with PTSD, and if you take the time and truly listen to what they have to say, and what they have been through, compassion would be the only natural response.

I have studied PTSD and anxiety in depth because I wanted to learn more about it. Through reading multiple books on the latest research, I am able to understand my diagnoses. Books have helped me to understand that I am not alone, and through them I have found tools that help me.

It became important for me to study the latest information on my diagnosis because of the new developments and research available every day. If I didn't understand my diagnosis, how could I help myself?

My college studies in psychology boosted my understanding. But I am a naturally curious person, and I love to read and wanted to understand: *what did it mean for me?*

Learning to deal with PTSD and anxiety shaped my new path. These feelings and their medical labels were foreign to me, and I had to learn how to cope in a healthy way. The physical exercise of walking and the creative exercise of art were helping me too slowly, almost at a glacial pace. I needed sharper tools to help put all those broken pieces back together. PTSD and anxiety were with me to stay, and it was out of my control. I couldn't be angry about it anymore. I just had to learn effective ways to handle it.

In my readings and through therapy, it came to me that I had to face my fear and walk right into one of the triggers of my pain. It helped me to clean out the nursery and donate all the baby items. Together my husband and I went in there and painted and created a new space. I don't know much about Feng Shui but it feels like that is what we did.

Magically I did not crumble with sadness when I walked by the room anymore! After we transformed the room, I did understand why the therapist had advised me to wait a month before opening that door. I did have to be a little stronger to do that process.

After going through this specific process, I learned to work with many different methods that I could integrate into my lifestyle. One of the best tools that have helped me is essential oils. Anyone who works with essential oils knows the benefits of them. My mother is amazing with essential oils. She works with experts in the field and has been kind enough to teach me a lot about them. So many gifts my parents have, and I don't take any of them for granted.

I realized that I have zero control of the flashbacks and the nightmares, that is just simply my brain processing everything. Years later I have learned what some of my triggers are. Triggers are the sight or smell of something that is going to trigger a memory. Mine are too personal to publish in a book, but to offer an example, at least I *can* walk through a baby section today and keep going. The anxiety still comes and it is a little more to handle. Little things like this that used to be easy for me, or once didn't affect me, do. *But in no way do I let them immobilize me.* I truly feel for people for are immobilized by anxiety and PTSD. If I could, I would create a magic bubble for all the people who suffer from both.

Do you know what it is like to have your heart race when

you are in a situation? Or when you can no longer handle crowds, due to the anxiety that it creates? Or the moment when you see something, or smell something, or touch something and every memory comes flooding back to you? And then *bam!!* You are back to relieving the same moment. It's like a really bad déjà vu movie playing in your head over and over again.

It's amazing how one little thing can bring the mind back in time—it seems quite unfair to me. I'm still trying to understand the human body and mind, and how it all functions. Do PTSD sufferers really need to relive every horrible moment they have been through? What is the purpose of that?

There are the simplest things that I see, which sometimes seem to move me back several steps in my healing. It's a deeply frustrating process, and I don't wish it on anyone.

Someone wise told me that "the minute you stop growing you become stagnant." I didn't fully understand these words until years later, but have passed on the information to other people who have been stuck in trauma. It makes sense that if someone is not willing to put the time and effort into their own growth, how could they possibly expect to get better?

In addition to having access to tools through my self-directed "continuing education" on PTSD and anxiety, my husband and I are fortunate to have a tremendous amount of emotionally supportive people in our lives. When life brings on the challenges (and it always does), it will truly tell you who your true friends are. To be able to pick up the phone and speak with a family member or good friend when I need it is priceless, and I am so grateful and appreciative of that.

In the year I went to university and finished my degree after a long hiatus, I really had to work through anxiety. Holy crap! Is college stressful!! Finishing one's degree is not a small obstacle. The constant demands, the deadlines, the forever logging into a system where you have to submit work to, the emails to keep up with, and the studying—who was the genius that thought of a clock running while you are taking a test online? I guarantee you it was not a sufferer of anxiety.

In my last semester, there was a moment in February where I was about to walk out due to the stress and anxiety. With my niece and nephews as my inspiration, I didn't. I looked at their photos in my study area to keep me motivated and on track. All four of their faces are what got me through.

Despite a full course load and a demanding schedule, I had to keep my anxiety at a normal level. I haven't stated it yet but I am Type 2 Diabetic, so I have to watch that too. Somehow in this situation, the anxiety seemed to drive me. I got assignments and studying done way before the deadline. Shout out to the professors who released assignments for a whole semester so I could work at my own pace. They are the ones helping the students who are go-getters that thrive with the freedom to work on their own. For someone who has anxiety, this helped me tremendously. One day I hope professors realize that not all students study well when receiving assignments one week at a time. Not all students function on the same level. I wish for more holistic approaches that honor the unique strengths of each student.

"Do you feel different since you graduated?" is a question people kept asking me after I got my degree. It seemed too early to tell, but I was sure of one thing: it's not like the core of who I am is changed overnight just because I was not holding a diploma. I do not believe anyone is a less of a person if they do not have a college degree. Some of the greatest people I know didn't graduate college and they are successful and all-around great people! My definition of a successful person is someone who is kind and compassionate and giving—they should give a degree for that!

For the years that I didn't have my degree, I encountered people who looked down on me, and some even vocalized, in no uncertain terms, that they were somehow better than me. My inner question was always, *how does their degree give them the right to treat people like shit and make them feel inferior?* Degree or no degree, it also has no bearing on how hard someone works. Some of the hardest-working people I have ever met don't have a degree and they are happy! They are running successful businesses, too.

Whether we have a degree or not, we have countless resources at our fingertips to educate us on what really matters to us, so that we can improve our health and the quality of our life. Through self-education, I have learned to slow down. Even though PTSD and anxiety are here to stay, I accept it now and take it step by step and breath by breath.

It's true, I was angry when I got dually diagnosed in 2008, but soon realized that it was another path for me. Life had changed its plans for me once again… and what could I do?

Plan A: Crawl up in a ball and shrivel up, or Plan B: say, "OK, new path, new plan... and here we go."

Plan B. I am that glass-half-full kind of woman.

Hugs to the people in the world who have anxiety and PTSD. I feel you and please know that you are not alone.

CHAPTER 6

My Love Affair with Food

Now there is a relationship for me that is always consistent, my personal relationship with food. Everybody who knows me *knows* I am a foodie. What they don't understand is that food for me is about being transported to another place and time, where there is a happy memory of the food that I am eating. My poor parents. Every time I visit them, I have to go to specific restaurants to taste all my favorite cuisines. Luckily, they indulge me and take me everywhere I want to eat. They live in a part of the United States known for its restaurants!! You can truly get a good bagel with lox and cream cheese, and the combination is a slice of heaven!!

I will be honest with you: when I was diagnosed with Type 2 Diabetes five years ago, I had to work hard to lose forty pounds and with a little luck (and with a lot of discipline) I hit my doctor's goal. No small journey there. Those of you who are diabetic know that food is something we think about every day. There is a genetic component to Type 2 Diabetes, but I own the fact that I wasn't too healthy five years ago. I can't blame my Diabetes on the lack of medical information due to being adopted. My healing is coming from acknowledging my part in all of it.

Which brings us to the love of food—what it means to me and how it fills my soul! Even though my love affair with it may have led to some health issues, I simply have to express my joy about it in the journey of rediscovering home. Because food can't be separated from the concept of home.

Imagine, for a moment, the smell of pizza, or the first bite of a cheeseburger when the cheese is melted to perfection and the fries are sizzling and crispy on your plate. Or when you're sick and the first sip of your mom's chicken soup warms you all over! Or when your house is filled with the aromatic smells of the holidays. Pumpkin pie rising smells like fall. Turkey on Thanksgiving! Is there really any better smell in the world? To take a bite of that meal on a visit home and you taste all your mother's foods—it all comes back to you, the memories of sitting around the table when we were younger.

When I smell matzah ball soup, it whisks me back to every family gathering and every holiday we ever spent together. Anyone who has made matzah balls knows what an art that is: cook them too long, they are rocks, but undercook them and they fall apart. I can still smell my *Bubby's* kitchen (*Bubby* is grandmother in Yiddish) kitchen during those precious holidays.

Now when I eat a bowl of matzah ball soup, and the steam is rising and the soup is perfection, I feel my mother's love. My best friend and I have an expression: "If you put the matzah ball out there, be ready for it to be out there!" meaning that when you say something, you probably can't take back what you said, so be prepared for the consequences of your words and actions. *Can you take the matzah ball back, metaphorically speaking of course?*

We all have experienced how smells transports us to another place or time, or remind us of certain people. On that note, there is nothing that has more meaning to me than the taste of a creamy, delicious cheesecake. Let me explain. My family was in the cheesecake business in New York City, and at every major life event, a cheesecake from that bakery graced our table. My grandfather's partner is still running the business. Unfortunately, this grandfather died when I was about eight. It was the first deeply devastating death I experienced. He was the sun, stars and moon to me, and cheesecake is my instant connection to him. In fact, it's so important to me, that when I did a fundraiser for India in Missouri, I called his partner and asked if he would donate two cheesecakes to the fundraiser. "Yes, of course," he said and sent them straight away. My grandfather would have been proud. It's amazing how just walking by the dessert table that night and seeing his cheesecake there filled me up. Plus, people in the Midwest were pretty psyched to try a real New York Cheesecake. Cheesecake is creamy perfection in one bite, but it's more about the instant connection and almost being with my grandfather all over again.

Can you have a love affair with pizza, especially after cheesecake? I can tell you *yes*, it's possible. Whenever I am sad or happy, pizza is my go-to comfort food. I find it really interesting that both of these polar opposite emotions trigger the sense that I need pizza. The elegant marina sauce and the melted mozzarella calls to me. A cheese pizza with lots of meats and veggies, please! What is it about this magical food, when I am curled up on the couch and about to start a movie—it's the beginning of a perfect night! For the pizza lovers out there, I'm sure it is one of your comfort foods too.

I have a memory of being with two friends in New York City, about to go to a Broadway play. They asked what I wanted for dinner before the show. I was like, *are you kidding me?* But here's what I really said. "I am in New York City, I need real pizza, where the grease drips down your arm and you have to fold it because it is so big!!" I remember this like it was yesterday, even though it happened twenty years ago. When we got off the train, we literally ran to the closest pizza place. I love the fact that these friends, even though they have it around them all the time because they live in New Jersey, still appreciated my excitement about it. Awww, *pizza*...thank you to whoever created it!

Now if I could roll around in a big bowl of pasta, I probably would. Why? Because it fills my soul and enlightens me to a whole new level. Doesn't matter what type of pasta it is, I think pasta might be embedded in my DNA. Being a diabetic, I do try to cook a lot more whole grain pasta. I am only stating this, because I can almost hear people saying, *a diabetic who loves pasta?*

So back to pasta. On my bucket list is a trip to Italy. I want to go to Italy for hundreds of reasons, but I'm sure pasta is one of them. I love that it is messy and doesn't have to perfect.

Also, it can be cooked a million ways. I seriously get bored in the kitchen sometimes trying to come up with new food to cook—anyone relate to this? I'm beyond thankful for all the recipes that are online.

I am one of those women who is lucky because I have husband who likes to cook—and pasta is one of his specialties. Pasta any way! A steaming hot lasagna with a Caesar salad and warm rolls fresh out of the oven. Is there anything better?

And there is another food, which I imagine many of you can relate to: the beloved cheeseburger. The combination of beef cooked to perfection between the toasted sesame-seed buns, with a kosher pickle and the cheese melted and smothered between an onion and tomatoes—yes, that one. If I died tomorrow, a cheeseburger would be my last meal. I'm specific about it. It has to have Heinz ketchup and *always* has to be accompanied with a hot, steaming plate of fries that are golden and crispy. As last meals go, I figure, that would send me to heaven with the first bite!

My family laughs because we will go to breakfast at about 9:00 a.m., and there I am ordering a cheeseburger while they are starting the day with eggs and oatmeal. One of my nephews recently asked me at a restaurant, "How is your belly ready for a cheeseburger at 9:00? Mine doesn't even wake up for lunch or dinner food till later!" I told him, my belly is always ready for a cheeseburger, and he smiled. Whenever I travel abroad, it is usually the first meal upon returning to the States. What on Earth could be better?

Maybe eating ethnic food. I love Greek, Italian, Spanish,

Japanese, and Cuban. I will always try new ethnic foods—they're like a passport to another country. Even if only for a little while, I am transported to places I have dreamed about my whole life. When a country's unique spice blends are filling my nose and tickling my taste buds, I am immediately satisfied.

And I will never have enough words for the next food, which is deeply embedded into my core. It's salty, crispy, can be carried anywhere and goes with pretty much everything. I love the simplicity of it, but I'm overjoyed about the taste of the one and only wonderful potato chip!! Really, do I need to say anything else? Can you have a sandwich without them? That would almost be sacrilegious. It is seriously a love affair I have had my whole life. Chips are always in the house, and they are a comfort food on countless levels. It is the crunch, the salt, and the overall the tactile experience of holding them on the verge of the first bite.

It's a shame how in the United States, we don't *dine* on food. Culturally we tend to eat it super fast and go on with our day or night. It's only at fancy dining establishments or during holidays when I believe we truly dine and taste our food. I'm grateful to have a family that is big into dining together, especially for Sunday brunch. To me, when you can combine lunch and breakfast together, then you know it's going to be a great day! Not to mention that you can have a steak and a Belgium waffle in the same meal. Aren't the best of food worlds coming together? Seriously, I look down and could cry at the sight of eggs Benedict with hollandaise sauce next to a steak, accompanied by a piece of sausage. Then there's the pasta with a nice crepe accompanied by a piece of bacon. Yummy! As you can tell, I'm a total carnivore. I'm one of those people who needs meat with a side of meat, and I hope any vegetarians and vegans will understand this is just part of my makeup. As such, brunch to me is one of those perfect eating experiences. Due to the fact that it is usually on Sunday, people will slow down. Love you bunches, brunch.

I hope you laughed and enjoyed sampling the foods that bring pure joy and love into my world, as much as I loved sharing them. There are others, too many to mention, that are important and have their place in my world, but I would not be a true foodie if I didn't ask you—what foods do you recommended?

And now, in the chapter ahead, we'll shift gears from flavors of food...

I aim to give your heart a taste of India.

CHAPTER 7

Healing My Heart in India

The first time I returned to India, I experienced bouts of grief associated with unresolved issues of the adoption and the miscarriage. But I also had this epic moment in India, which helped me in a way that you can't even imagine.

The orphanage I came from, Family Village Farm, is a truly special place. In Tamil, it is called *Mudhiyor Balar Kudumba Grama Panni* (translation: Elderly Children Family Village Farm), located in the state of Tamil Nadu in Kasam, India. You will quickly come to appreciate why the words Elderly and Children are included in its name.

Family Village Farm is a place that rescues children, women and the elderly. The room mothers help take care of the children. There are grandmothers who help to raise the children as well. These women have either been abandoned or widowed, and they were all taken in too and given a good home. This was the primary mission of the founder, Dr. Pauline E. King, when she established it. Dr. King is the woman who took me in and cared for me for months. The orphanage has an incredible school, which the children attend until they graduate high school. It is so well run that unless you see it in action, you can't imagine it or comprehend it.

People there have touched my soul in ways that have changed my life forever. As you can imagine, with the orphanage being my first home, it is a place I look for clues and information about my heritage. Recently one of the directors emailed me: "There are still people here who know and remember you when you were here, but please be aware that they are getting older." I took his message to heart. I felt lucky because I did find people who remembered me and could tell me things, about my first eleven months in India.

The year 2013 turned out to be "my time" to research my life and begin filling in all the missing pieces of this puzzle called my life. I am still working on the puzzle, and if I don't get the whole puzzle solved, it's OK because *it is a big puzzle!* My heart is grateful for the people who are helping me to put the puzzle together, including the countless hours some of them are spending on my behalf. Your efforts are so appreciated. One person in particular has been going door to door in hopes of finding my family members. And some of family members in India have prayed for me to reconnect and have supplied me with irreplaceable pieces of evidence of existence in India. I love them all so much.

Lots of people have asked me, "Why don't you just work on it from the States?" Easier said than done. I have to be there with my feet planted in my birthright country and work with the people directly. Email is wonderful, but a lot in this world of technology and communication is lost in translation. It is a process where I have to go through files and go to locations where I once was. As overwhelming and daunting as this process is, it helps me. Even as I search through files upon files for one small clue to my life in India, it cannot be accomplished without me being there physically.

I might not learn things every time I search a new location, but somehow being inside a new room where I was as a baby helps me so much. It's a connection to a moment in my life, whether or not the time was short, whether or not I can remember it.

One time, I visited a hospital where I had been as a baby, at a time when I had been very sick. Just being in that hospital was a significant moment for me. It is a world-renowned hospital, where the doctors and the staff are seriously the hardest-working people in the medical field that I have ever seen. These are true physicians and nurses who are there to help people heal, and not to just cash a paycheck. These professionals are so dedicated to their patients, I didn't know that type of care existed! I also spent many days at the orphanage, an especially healing place for me. It could be the people, the music, the dancing, the food, and the kids. It could be hearing the laughter from the kids that radiates through the air. It could be the wholeheartedly devoted staff, which gives it 150 percent! It could be the overall structure—both the buildings and the operations laid out in precise detail. It's highly scheduled, as it would have to be working with over two-hundred kids.

How can I do justice when I talk about these children? They are remarkable! Despite having come from the worse situations possible, they are thriving in light of the care and love that is provided to them. This is all made possible by the staff and donors to the organization that supports the Family Village Farm—how could I ever thank them enough?

I have seen with my own eyes how much the Family Village Farm family deeply appreciates all the help. The children range from babies up to the age of eighteen, for whom the adults have created the most loving and nurturing environment possible. From the grandmothers to the room mothers to the people who work in the office, to all the teachers who work at the school daily, and all the staff overseeing operations, this place is an authentic success in its capability to care for these children.

The school is larger than you might think—it is not just the children from the orphanage, but also children who are bussed in from outside areas. I have spent time in the school and have been amazed at what they are learning. Their curriculum is incredible.

The volunteer programs, in which I participated during my visit, blew my mind too. People come from nations across this world to volunteer at Family Village Farm and at the school. The children love meeting people from outside countries; better than the Internet, it is their exposure to the outside world.

My connection to the children runs deep and fills my heart in ways no one can fathom, for I once was one of them. The children and I connected very fast; they had been told I was part of that community coming home, yet it seemed they sensed it with their hearts too. We played and laughed and cooked together. The teenagers taught me cricket (I still need more lessons). A person who has not had two different homes might not understand what this feels like, but try to imagine it. If you have two families, you understand it.

More than a family, it's a community for all ages that embraces anyone who enters with nurturing on so many levels. You have the grandmothers, who are teaching me a lot, to the mothers who are caring for the children, and the staff who are dedicating their love to this place.

Some of the grandmothers, room mothers and staff have been there over twenty-five years. Of course, when I first met them, they had a lot of questions! Indian people are deeply curious and like to learn a lot about other people.

"So are you married?"

"Yes, I've been married for years."

"Do you have kids?"

I responded that my body was not able, putting my hand on my stomach so they could understand.

They did. But one thing they couldn't comprehend is how it is that my husband and I live in the Midwest, while our families live on the East Coast. It's hard to explain the cultural differences between the two countries, but I try my best to share from my experience to help expand their world the way they expand mine, even as we work through the nuances of language and translation.

You see, in this area of India the people speak Tamil. It is the language of Tamil Nadu, but there are other languages spoken in Tamil Nadu: *Telugu, Kannada, Urdu and Malayalam*. But they all speak English, the children up to the moms. It is usually the older generation that struggles with English. I have learned how to make it work; I always have a teenager translate for me. Also, there are amazing Tamil Apps that have helped me too. But really, there is no language barrier for me when I travel to India. If you know India's history, you know the British have played a huge part. Yet my greatest epiphany on that trip did not involve words at all.

Leading up to this healing moment, I was walking with one of the staff women who is responsible for running many programs. She is so tall, especially next to me, and everything about her is kind and gracious; she has only pure intentions. A really hard worker, she has devoted her life to helping these children at the orphanage. This was 2013, but I can see this moment today, because it was so crucial and it is embedded in my brain.

From the office down to the school is about half a mile in distance, and together we were trotting along the dirt country road, with cars, and bikes, and motorcycles and people coming and going. Again, this is India there are people everywhere. And of course cows are everywhere too. Cows are sacred in India—for people who don't know that fact, I wanted to share that—and their being everywhere is a reminder of the sacred in the everyday. Despite the details of the busy scene, I even remember what she was wearing. It was the most beautiful sari, red crimson in color with an orange marmalade scarf wrapped around her neck, her long gold earrings dangling and decorating her face. India is so colorful—there are colors I have seen there that I have not seen anywhere else!

As we approached the school, two country roads split, one going right and the other heading into the entrance of the school. There we stood chatting. She was facing me and a mountain range filled the horizon behind her on the border between Tamil Nadu and Andhra Pradesh.

She asked me, "Do you have kids?"

"No," I said and explained why. She made a face of compassion and kindness, and then smiled—she has a smile that makes you smile; it is so bright and happy, and contagious.

She looked at me, and said, "Yes, you have kids."

And of course I made a face of complete bewilderment.

She continued, "How blessed you are... you have over 150 children who you will connect with and love and carry in your heart. As, they will carry you in their heart as well."

It was my second day in India and that moment of listening to her with the warm sun shining and the mountains behind her opened my heart, which had suffered so much loss and pain. Right then, I felt it slowly coming to life in a very powerful way. I hugged her and thanked her. The gratefulness I feel for her and her words that day—it still overwhelms me in a positive way.

That afternoon, I had more conversations with the teenage girls, who rock by the way. I had so much fun with them, and still do. They called me their sister, and I called them mine. My dream of Indian sisters I had wished for my whole life... had come true. They knew I loved them too. While we were walking to dinner, we were singing and dancing and skipping along our way. They asked me about being married and whether or not I had children. As I explained, they stopped, about six of them and me, and made a circle and we all held hands. And they beautifully responded, "You have us and always will." They all hugged me and said they were sorry that I didn't have kids, but reassured me to the fact that they would always be there for me.

Off we went to dinner, and my heart opened again.

Whenever I visit the orphanage, I spend a lot of time with the teenagers, especially when there is a huge group of volunteers visiting. I try to give them extra attention—not that they need it, yet I am sensitive to the fact that people love to be in the nursery with the young ones. I always ask them what they want from the States and try to fulfill a lot of their wish list while I am there—for example, sports equipment and movies. All the kids love movies but they been watching the same movies for years. So when I returned in 2015, I brought new movies, kindly donated by a lot of my friends. Thank you to my friends who helped me with a DVD drive; the children were thrilled!

The teenagers are also always up for adventure. Remember the mountain that splits the two states, which I described? I went to hike it with thirty-plus kids, all guiding me up the mountain. Off we went, their sole mission to get me up to the top of the mountain. They were in front and back of me, to make sure I was safe. We started at the bottom and they moved the brush out of my way as I walked.

The boys were highly respectful, true gentlemen, and the girls were there with me, right by my side. We walked a path and then started to climb. I was in awe of the kids—they were experts in climbing this mountain! We laughed and chatted the whole way, and some were even videotaping as I ascended the mountain. Up I went, surrounded with laughter and joy and happiness doing this with the kids. Step by step, they guided me on the path. I am proud to say I made it up about three-quarters of the way before I decided it was time for me to rest.

I'll never forget watching the kids who continued on all the way up to the top. Others sat with me and we chatted and took in the sunset over the mountains. We had to descend before it got dark, but we sat there for one amazing moment. I had picked some flowers on the way up the mountain and left some there as a memorial to people I have lost, and in honor of a dear friend who had lost both her parents. Here on the top of the mountain, I was sitting with my Indian family in deep peace. They guided me down safely, and we made it down before it got dark.

When we returned to the base, they said, "Don't worry and be disappointed you didn't make it to the top, you will do it on the next trip, and it's a hard mountain to climb!"

Little did they realize that climbing the mountain was another moment of my heart healing. I smiled at them and said, "All the way to the top next time!"

During my visit, I not only spent quality time with the children… I had to hang out with my grandmothers! Usually, after I had chia tea in the morning, it was off to them before breakfast, to sit, chat and do girl things. Mostly we did hair and laughed. They asked all about beauty products in the United States, and I learned about Indian beauty products in turn. They taught me *all* the tricks on how to manage Indian hair and Indian skin, which can be summed up in two words: coconut oil! Now there are lots of palm trees in India and someone is always willing to climb up the trees and get fresh coconuts. They use all of the coconut, for food and dry skin issues and for perfecting hair. Let me say, that I am not a person who shops organically but to me that this is what life should be—the definition of organic for your body and soul.

Two of the grandmothers knew me when I was baby. I had a strange experience during the first two days with one of them. Every time I walked by her, she would just stare at me and I couldn't figure out why. She was looking at me as if I were a ghost. Then I found out the reason why. She had a daughter who died, and she said I was the spitting image of her daughter. She and I got so close. She would look into my eyes and squeeze my cheeks with pure affection and love. The fun times we shared cannot be adequately described. Both grandmothers were able to tell me stories of my time in India, and how I was cared for. It was, and is, so reassuring. There is a grandfather who knew me as well, and he told me stories too. What a blessing the elderly hearts are to me. I believe that you can learn from all age groups.

I also sat with the grandmothers when they prayed, as I do each time I visit. Every day they pray for the world, as the children do. They sit on carpet and the sound like a symphony when they pray. Then we sit in circle and talk, just being women enjoying and learning from each other. What they teach me is invaluable—they embody wisdom from every stage of life.

Is it natural to have issues with adults who forget that they were kids at one time? Some people seem to think children have nothing to offer them; it is sad and I have seen it too many times. The elder generation has been though *everything* and has so much knowledge to pass on, if only we take the time to listen.

The people are the heartbeat of Family Village Farm. It's hard to pin a finger on what makes it such a special place because it's not any one thing, it's everything you sense on the premises. It's the love that is felt everywhere there. It's the sounds in the air filled with laughter and music. It's the scent of cumin and curry, and the smell of the fires burning in in the morning. It the aroma of jasmine and the pitter-patter of feet moving around with a purpose. It's the taste of the simmering hot chai tea that fills your soul, as you awaken to a new day and a whole new way of being.

CHAPTER 8

My Near-Death Experiences

I have this "thing"—I don't want to waste my time on this Earth. Beyond a shadow of a doubt I know that, when I die, that I will have checked off everything on my bucket list.

How that will happen, I have no idea.

Every January to this point, I have written my bucket list and accomplished nothing on it. It truly pisses me off. In many respects, the years have been like a bad song that keeps playing through my mind over and over again. I'm laughing now because I just wrote a list for this year, and I'm wondering if I'll get anything done on it. I hope so.

Once I was speaking with my godfather, who said to me, "You and your husband work really hard but please make time to do the things that you want to do, before it's too late. Live your lives, and have no regrets." I truly took his words to heart and they are the reason that I am now living my bucket list. This book is a perfect example; I have always wanted to write a book, but life got in the way. *"Now is the time."* I hear his words in my head. *"Live your life."*

From now on, every year I am going to do at least three

things on my list. Why am I so determined? Because I have had two near-death experiences. Next I will describe each one, along with how they have taught me to not waste a day and to not take life for granted. Again I am not a deeply religious person, but I am spiritual and had profound experiences that I can't explain, other the connection that I have with my husband. I truly believe that someone was watching over me.

During my first brush with death, I was vacationing in Mexico with my aunt, mom and cousin. The four of us live far away from one another, so to make up for lost time we do the mother-and-daughter trips every couple of years. This time we were hanging at my aunt's place, enjoying the sun and pool. Her house backs against the Pacific Ocean and there are no words to describe the view. It's spectacular. The ocean shines and sparkles, radiating the color emerald. It was one of those days that I like to describe as "a perfect day."

These women are some of my most favorite people in the world. My mom, my cousin and I wanted to head down to the rocks to get a better view of the ocean. There is no beach there, just rocks, and on this day there was a ridiculously strong current. The two of them were behind me, and I was sitting out on one of the rocks, just touching my feet in the water. I spent a lot of my life playing in the Atlantic Ocean and never really spent a lot of time in the Pacific Ocean. The day before this one was actually my first time swimming in the Pacific.

So I was dangling a foot in the ocean to feel the temperature. I had not realized the moss-covered rocks were *very* slippery. I had no intentions at all of going into the ocean, given the unforgiving current and the rocks were everywhere. I had taken oceanography and understood currents, rip tides, undertows and other aspects of the ocean. Anyone who dared to go in would be bounced around like a tennis ball. Now I love the ocean, everything about it. But I am also a person who respects the its power.

People tend to forget that when we jump in the ocean, we are the visitors and that we are not in our natural habitat. I say this as a water lover and strong swimmer who adores playing in the waves, snorkeling or just having fun walking the beach. The experience that I am about to describe has not changed that at all.

So I was sitting on the rocks, a huge wave came up, and I slipped off the rocks. It was *almost* like being on a water slide right into the ocean. To help you understand what happened next, I am going to describe the rocks—sharp and everywhere. The waves were coming in and out, the way waves do. I fell into a hole where the water would rush in and out, and the hole was encircled by rocks. It was like being sucked into a vortex. Down I went, as the waves came in and out.

My body had been sucked down to the bottom of the ocean, but I could not touch the ocean floor. I was in a tube of rocks and water. As the water rushed back out to the ocean, I was sucked down further and further still as the waves came back to the shore. It was like being inside a geyser where the water has pressure building and skyrockets into the air. That kind of pressure.

So there I was in this hole, pushed back down again, to the

bottom, and twice skyrocketed again. Meanwhile my mom and my cousin were watching it all unfold. There was no way they could rescue me; they would have fallen in too. So then came third time, where I was pushed back down with an extreme force. Exhaustion was setting in. Yes, the rules of physics were at work all around me.

I focused on the fact that when I was pushed up, I had to remember to breathe and get as much air as I could. Meanwhile, I was getting cut up by the rocks, and blood was coming from my hands and arms. As I was pushed to the bottom, I would try to grab onto something; naturally I feared that I was going to be swept out to the ocean. On the bottom that third time, I held on really hard to the rocks and my legs were propelled in front of me. I was still holding on to a rock.

What happened next was amazing: some kind of cave appeared where there was no light coming in and I was realized there would be no way out. So I let my body relax, which felt nearly impossible to do in those kinds of conditions. Fight or Flight had kicked in and I'm not sure but I think my adrenaline was in overload; the ability of the human body, and how it functions, never ceases to amaze me.

So there I was and this sense of peace and calm washed over me. This was it. I was going to drown in the Pacific Ocean. It was going to be a violent death, because the rocks would break my bones, and the water would drown me. Yet, I was calm and peaceful. It might be because I love the ocean, and if that was where I was going to die, I accepted it. How that was possible, I still have no idea?

Holding on to the rocks, I felt ready to give up and die. Then somehow, miraculously I saw my husband's face and I could hear his words. My husband was home in the Midwest. The words I heard were the following: "Kick one more time for me, kick one more time!" I could see his face and hear his words as if he were standing in front of me. So I let go of the rocks and swam really hard, and reached a hand out into the air. Then another hand grabbed mine and pulled me to safety.

My aunt's friend had just arrived at the house and he asked where we were. She said we were at the rocks, and he quickly came down to check on us. Being from the area, he knew the rocks were dangerous. This man was so strong, he lifted me up with *one* hand.

He had saved my life!

Once I got out, we went up to my aunt's house and they checked me over. My mom applied essential oils all over my cuts. I was shaken up, but within an hour I was back in the pool playing with my cousin. That morning my mom was not going to bring her oils, but something told her to bring it. Thank God she did! They played a major role in healing my cuts and calming my nerves. Moms are rock stars—they always know what their kids need.

I am going to take another minute here to thank the man who saved my life. We took him out to dinner and thanked from the bottom of our hearts, for what he did for me. *Can you thank someone enough for saving your life?* Cheers to the man who saved my life. There are no words to tell you how appreciated you are. But I will tell you this: I will not waste my life and will help as many people as I can. You were an angel that saved me when I needed to be saved. I think of you often, and hope to see you again.

Being a non-religious person, how do I explain the fact that I saw my husband's face and heard his words? I have no idea how to explain that and I don't know if I have to understand it all. It was what gave me the strength to kick one more time, and I'm glad I did.

The next near-death experience was also eye-opening and life-changing for me. I already mentioned I am a Type 2 diabetic. What I have not told you was that this diagnosis saved my life. I had been really sick with the flu with a fever of 102 for several days. Running a high fever is not uncommon for me at all, so I didn't too think much of it. My mom told me that I suffered febrile seizures when I was little before I grew out of it. But I am still one of those people who runs a fever in the range of 102- to 104, however usually not for many days.

I had been going back and forth back to the doctor, and nothing seemed to be working for me. I went to the hospital for more tests. After I was admitted, the staff ran multiple tests. I was not going to leave without knowing the underlying cause of the fever; it seemed fair to ask that much.

It was about 11:45 at night when the nurse came in with lab results for my CBC (complete blood count). She immediately put me on the phone with the doctor.

I'll never forget the nurse; she was so kind and compassionate. The doctor told me I had Type 2 Diabetes, and that my blood sugar was way too high. It was so severe that if I had not gotten help, there was a possibility of having had severe diabetic complications. I sat on the edge of the hospital bed, breathing in their every word.

Having sent my husband home to get rest, I called him and spoke with him and my immediately family. Then I asked the nurse if I could be alone to process everything. I was mad at the diagnosis, but I was madder at myself. I didn't know anything about Diabetes up to this point. In my head, it was one more way of my body failing me.

At midnight, I cried for about ten minutes and then got it together. I had my iPad and starting researching as much as I could. The nurse gave me a lot of information, too. The next day my husband and I met with multiple people and found out about a Diabetes class, which the hospital strongly recommended. I took the class and learned everything I needed to care for myself.

I will be forever grateful that I had a mysterious flu that inspired me to speak up, seek a second opinion, and demand answers. Use your voice, and be strong, and be your own patient advocate.

And there you have my NDEs (a well-known abbreviation for near-death experience). So what did I take away from the situations? To make the most of life. To not waste it. To find true meaning in life, and to be grateful. The older generation I have been around has told me, "It goes too fast, so make the best of it." Now in my forties, I feel like it is going very fast. Like I held onto the rocks and kicked, now I hold onto the people I love and do the things I want to before it's too late.

Before closing this chapter, I have one more story to share with a valuable life lesson on how cell phones can save your life. In 2008, I stood outside on my driveway on a bitter-cold February morning. On my way to meet my parents for breakfast, I was brushing snow off the car. Our driveway has a slant, and it was beyond icy. I still can feel how cold it was, the kind of cold that rips through your bones.

I had the car running, which you do in the Midwest in the winter. So I had thrown my purse in the car, but put my cell phone in my back pocket. My boots helped to stabilize me to a point, but as I slipped on the ice, I could hear my ankle and leg break. For people who have been through that, it is a sound that is unforgettable. It makes me cringe even today.

My body had fallen behind the front tire. I was beyond terrified. Not to mention the fact, that there was no one out on my heavily trafficked street. We live on an extremely busy street, with lots of cars and walkers and joggers, but no one was out there that day and the pain was beyond intolerable. *Luckily*, I had my cell phone in my pocket and was able to call my parents, who were less than a mile away at the time.

I don't even know if they could understand me. I also called 911 and had the nicest person on the phone. She said, "Do you hear the ambulance and the fire truck?"

"Yes," I responded while screaming in pain. Within five minutes or less, they were there and so were my husband and parents. My biggest fear was that the car might roll over me and kill me. The EMTs hoisted me up on a stretcher and rushed me to the hospital. They repeatedly told me that my cell phone being in my pocket saved my life. They always advise people to keep them in their pocket, because accidents often when people are alone. Had I not had my phone, my body would have gone into shock due to the brutal temperatures that day.

I had an emergency surgery that night. My leg was dislocated and bones in my ankle and leg were broken. Pins and lots of metal were put in to fix it. I'm still so grateful to my amazing orthopedic surgeon. It was nine months of recovery and physical rehab. I'm sharing this with you to highlight, among the other life-and-death lessons I have learned, that a cell phone can be a life-saving device. Of course, it can also be a diversion from what really matters in life. With our phones, like words, what matters is the intention behind how we use them.

CHAPTER 9

Fitting In in America: Does America Love Me?

Across the country, I'm an invited speaker on the issue of diversity awareness. The reason is: I am an Indian Jewish woman. This is not common, and when I speak I share my experiences on how cruelly I've been treated based on my skin color and religion, it wakes people up to the fact that *racism still exists* in our country and cultivates compassion for all as they walk a mile in my shoes. My speaking career began twelve years ago, when I was invited by a friend who is a college professor to speak to her students. She asked me to share my particularly unusual angle of the sadly not uncommon story of racism in America. I have enjoyed giving many talks since then.

My purpose is to educate people about the effects of racism and to create awareness where people don't believe it is going on. I confess that I am a not a lover of public speaking. I get nervous before each speech, as I am sure you understand. But I face the fear and do it anyway, focused on my goal that everyone listening will leave with open eyes and an open heart. In one particular talk I gave at a college, I received a question that

I at first didn't know how to answer. I will share the shocker of a question, and you'll understand why I had to think about it, after I lay the foundation of my experiences.

Growing up, for me, was pretty much about not fitting in. I was not African-American and I was not white. Racism issues began when I left the comfort of a private school setting and headed into the trenches of public schools. It was hard for me to find my place. Everyone knows how cliquish high school is. It's challenging enough to fit in to begin with and for anyone in the minority, it's even harder. At least that was my experience.

The middle and high school years were a particularly dark time for me and I couldn't wait to get out of there. I even graduated early so I could. We must remember to have compassion for young people who are going through middle school and high school, as those years are very difficult socially and emotionally. I hear horror stories from friends who have kids in this age group: the bullying, the impact social media has had on their children, and the downright cruelty people have experienced.

After I left the hell that was high school, I ventured down to the Southern United States for college. I felt lucky because I went to a college that was extremely diverse, and it allowed me to fall in love with school again. I started school in my twenties and completed my degree much later after life circumstances moved me to the Midwest. The instances of racism that occurred in the South and Midwest had nothing to do with universities I attended; they arose in interactions with certain people in the general population.

Everything that I am about to share occurred over a twenty-year period, starting in my early twenties. And although these events occurred in the Southern and Midwestern United States, racism in my personal experiences *is not limited* to specific regions of the United States.

I am going to paint a picture of what I like to call "the worst I have seen." Perhaps these problems are exacerbated by the fact that I am only 5'3" and people tend to feel that they can be intimidating with me because of my size. I *do not* engage when someone crosses a line, please understand that. Most of the situations that I am about to describe have transpired with complete strangers.

I am not intending to focus on the worst in people, because moments of darkness can reveal the most exquisite light. In a number of situations, kind people have stood up for me. Then there were other times when people have just sat there and stared and didn't say anything. Why? If you see someone being harassed, no matter the reason, speak up! Don't just stand there and watch and add to the whole bystander effect unless it would put people in danger. Just standing there is not OK. I love my country a lot, but I have often wondered, *does it love me?*

And now for the question that stunned me during one of my presentations: a student raised her hand and asked, "If people are so mean to you in this country, why don't you just leave America?" At first, I truly didn't know what to say to her. I had never been asked this question during the Q&A part at the end of my speeches, where I invite people to ask me questions, and I always answer honestly, with the intention of creating a healthy and safe conversation with the power to eradicate any stereotypes that people have.

Drawing a deep breath, I responded, "I love America and I'm proud to be American." I stand by those words, even when these have been some of my experiences:

- **"Great, an n-word and a kike (bad word for a Jewish person) all wrapped in one.**" I was playing football with friends, and this was when a man who weighed about 225 approached me and said this. Caught like a deer in the headlights, I felt lucky when my cousin protected me. I was wearing my Jewish Star. After that occurred, I stopped wearing it for a long time. I felt angry at the fact, that I could not feel safe wearing my Jewish Star. Jews have sacrificed enough and have been through too much, and there is no reason why we should still feel unsafe in this country. Now, I only put it on where I feel it is safe to do so. But shouldn't we be able to feel safe all of the time?

- **"You can't afford to shop in our establishment."** I was shocked. The sales person truly came up and said that to me as I was buying a gift for my mom and dad, and was super excited about what I had found. They had just moved in to a new house and it would have been their housewarming gift. I asked to speak to the manager, who behaved no better than the sales person. Neither rang me up or asked to run my credit card. I left disheartened. I would never patronize an establishment where the employees talk to people that way.

- **"What *are* you?"** I have heard that multiple times in life. *What do you mean, what am I?* I am a human being just like you! I have no issues when people ask, "Where do you come from?" That is a respectful alternative.

- **"You can't possibly live in this neighborhood."** This has happened to me multiple times across the United States. Once a cop followed me all the way to my childhood home, because he didn't believe I lived there. I felt terrified, that my parents were going to think that I did something wrong, given that I was sixteen years old and being followed by the cops to the front door. My father was amazing! He said, "She does live here, and please don't follow my daughter again." I don't think the cop knew what to do because my father is white, and he was surprised by that.

- **"You can't come in here."** This was said to me by a bank teller after I had already stepped up to the window. In this situation, I requested to speak with the manager about his employee's racial-profiling behavior. He was cordial and assured me that the bank had a zero tolerance for that.

- **"I'll call you brown girl."** I stood in a national pharmacy, where I had been a customer for years. A new employee asked me where I was from. When I responded, "I am from

India," she said, "I'll call you brown girl." The line of people behind me just stood there staring at me. I left feeling upset. A week later, I came across her again. She was unaware that I was friends with her boss and manager and I gave her a chance to apologize. I asked her to refer to me, by Mrs. and my last name. She replied, "But you are brown." I repeated myself again and she got the point. How can I speak on diversity awareness, if I don't do my part to be clear with people about how I want to be treated?

These are just a few examples that I share not to complain, but to shed light on the experience of being a minority in America. May we all remember the person sitting next to us may be from a very different background, and have many gifts and talents to offer. Just because we are different doesn't mean we can't get along. May we all aspire to live in this world without racism and hate. May we all remember that we can make a difference by standing up for those who are being mistreated.

I'll never accept the fact that some people hate me for my skin color and religion. What I can do is educate people, the best way I know how.

I have been asked, "How are you not angry and mad all the time?"

"What would that accomplish?" I reply. I don't group together one person's bad behavior with the entire race that represents that person.

I am an Indian Jewish woman married to a Christian German man. Our families love each other and get along.

Our family is diverse, with other adopted people in our family. I pray for the rest of the world to get along the way we do. As I continue to grow and discover my voice, I will continue to stand up for myself and share my experience to help bring about a positive evolution in the way people treat one another. That is the most important service I can offer this world.

CHAPTER 10

Love and the Heart of the Adopted

Love is perhaps the main reason why we do things. Love is universal. It is something all of us need and want. It is what we look for. It is why we keep our relationships going. It is how we hold our families and friends, and our wonderful pets, in our hearts.

Love is what this world needs more of. If we were to focus on love, and not hate, we would go a long way. Being that I am a deeply emotional person, I am driven by love. I lead with my heart and my brain catches up with me. Love is something that should never be taken for granted.

I am no expert in love. I had horrible past boyfriends and didn't know what love was till I met the man I married. He is the man of my dreams, and I don't take that for granted at all. I am being brutally honest in saying that I had no self-esteem in my twenties and my past-relationship record definitely reflects that. From my teens until my wedding day, I went through periods in my life when I was single and in relationship—either way, I was following a conditioned pattern where my self-esteem was based on what other people thought of me. It wasn't until I started working on myself that I found an ounce of self-esteem; only then was I in a place where I realized *I deserved love.*

When I say love is one of the most important things in the world, I'm not just talking about love in a couple relationship—I'm talking about the broader term which motivates to us to do good things. For example, my love for my three nephews and niece is what kept me motivated to finish my degree, as I was determined to be a role model for them.

The love of our families—that's a big one. There is not anything in this world that I wouldn't do for my family. If ever they needed me, I would be on the next plane to help them, and I know they would do the same for me.

Family is interesting. Either they shape you in a positive or negative way. Many of my friends have had childhoods that were beyond horrific. Yet some of them are now taking care of their aging parents, the same parents who made their lives a living hell. I asked one of them why she was doing it. Her response was, "I love them." She continued to tell me, "I know I will leave this world, knowing I did right by them, even though they didn't do right by me."

In my last semester in college, I studied family in depth and was amazed to learn all the dynamics and cultural differences within a family. Class discussions centered on the issues that are wrapped around the social unit we call a "family." This class depended heavily on opinions, as everyone brought personal childhood experiences to the roundtable. There were a lot of debates. Still through the discussions, one thing was clear: *love is the key to a successful family.*

Love guides us in all of our decisions. If we have no love for ourselves, can we truly love someone else? Why is that people often have a hard time loving themselves? Is it because self-love is so wrapped up in our self-esteem? In my life experience, my identity is so intertwined into my self-esteem that they almost go hand in hand. I truly admire and learn from people who love themselves and have good self-esteem.

Love, in my eyes, cannot clearly be defined—it is fluid, and it shifts and changes. It grows for a person as we get closer. Friendships grow the more we get to know someone. The love we feel for our spouses or partners grows more and more. Love doesn't have to be declared on Valentine's Day. I appreciate the ways my husband and I express love in words and action all year long versus the one day that lands on February 14th. There are many things we can do to express love to people who we are close to., and I'm not talking about buying people things; I'm talking about being there for people when they need you. That, to me, is the true definition of love.

I volunteer for certain organizations because of the love I have for them and the people they help. It's the love that drives me. Love can be a wonderful motivator and can bring out the best in people... and at the polarity, it can also appear to drive people to do the unthinkable. But that is not love—it is confusion. In a relationship where one person dominates the other, there is a layer of confusion. Such behavior is never ok, as we all know what it leads to. This confusion is the shadow of love. It is a sign that people have not yet learned to love and respect each other because they have not yet learned to love themselves.

No matter if someone calls it love, it is *not* love when someone talks down to another person or makes them feel inferior. It was my wonderful husband who taught me that, and I love him for that. He reaffirmed in me what my heart already knew—that love is respectful and kind. Again I experienced some terrible relationships beforehand because I didn't believe that I was worth more.

Someone asked me once, "What did you learn from your ex?" I quickly responded with, "How not to be treated!" Is there always a lesson to be learned from our past? Do the mistakes we made about love ultimately make us better people?

When it comes to finding self-love, how do we accomplish that? I can't count how many people for whom my wish is: may they see in themselves what I see in them. Self-doubt and low self-esteem clouds their perception of who they are. Having been there (and still being there sometimes), I have compassion and hope for them, that they see the beauty that radiates from them… they are so much more beautiful than what their inner critic is telling them.

How do we hush the inner critic? Where do we find inner love? I have about wondered these things my whole my life.

Being relinquished as a baby, even if the reason was to save my life, still makes me feel that I was not loved by my birth father. Someone told me that was not the case and I am still processing and working on all of it. My father, who loves me and raised me, was wonderful and still is—my feelings about my birth father are completely distinct. Doesn't it make sense that this degree of rejection as a baby would follow someone around their whole life? My struggle with self-worth seems to come down to the moment I was relinquished.

I have heard similar questions asked by other adopted people too, but these questions are my own: *Why was I given away? Was I not good enough for them to love me? What do babies do wrong? Could I have done something differently for them to have loved me more? Why didn't any of my extended family want me? Did they know about me? What did I do wrong? Did I cry too much? Did I not smile enough? Was I too costly? Was I not pretty enough? Did my births mother's death cause anyone to hate me? Do you wonder what it would be like if we ever met?*

Am I only an afterthought? Or is one of those situations where if I am out of sight, I am out of mind? Do you not realize that if I could fix what you disliked about me, I would have and would do that? Do you not think that I don't blame myself enough for my birth mother's death? She died giving me life. I live with the guilt that it was my fault.

How do you love yourself with constant uncertainty rolling around in your head? How can you love yourself when you were rejected at a young age? Is love something that we learn early and the rest of our life decisions are based on early experiences? What if you had no control of the beginning of your life, which all babies don't?

I share my inner struggles in hopes that it will help people understand what might be going through the minds and hearts of the adopted people they meet. I know a lot of people who adopted kids, and have observed these three things as a common thread in multiple conversations with adoptive parents:

1. **"I wish I knew the biological family, maybe it would explain my daughter or son better."** Maybe they don't need to be explained. Maybe they just need love and compassion. Keep in mind that since you have no biological connections to your child, if you changed you expectation of what he or she should be, then the outcome could be different. From the adoptee's perspective, of course we want answers to why we act the way we do; but since we can't know this, unconditional acceptance is all we need.

2. **"How do I fix them?"** Maybe they don't need to be fixed and should be accepted for who they are. Adopted kids are supposed to assimilate to the new family. Does the new family assimilate to them at all? Where is the compassion and love in this? I have heard the "fix" comment a lot, and it does not sit well with me. But in retrospect, all these conversation have transpired with nothing more than love and respect. It's an open and honest discussion with the ability for all of us to express thoughts and for those thoughts to be respected. This type of safe space for authentic communication is what an adoptee needs.

3. **"My adopted child…"** I have shared with parents that "if you just called them your child, it might open the door to a better connection with your child." My parents *never once* referred to me as the adopted

child. They introduced and still introduce me as their daughter. If people ask if I'm adopted, that's a different story. Of course people ask us that... I am Indian, and they are white!

One of the reasons why were are so close—or why I have allowed them to get so close to me—is because *they never made me feel like an outsider.* I am their daughter, period, the end. They are my parents, not my adoptive parents. My parents had the goal of adopting a child because there were so many kids in this world that needed a home. They succeeded, due to the fact that I never once in my 40+ years felt like an outsider.

What if when we raised our children, we allowed them more freedom to decide their future, and to fully express themselves, not within the bounds of what we think they "should" be? What if the possibility of pure and unconditional love for the future children of this world begins with us?

When I visit the children at the orphanage where I once lived, I have nothing but pure love and unconditional respect for them. I would like to see adults survive as well as some of the children have. I have seen the power of love in this place. It is the love from the grandmothers, mothers, staff, and others that is helping to raise over 150 children. Love is what is guiding these children.

We all notice when beauty radiates from people who are humble and beautiful inside. I believe in empowering children in hopes they develop a good self-esteem and radiate such beauty. Society places a ridiculous amount of pressure on children to grow up and fit in—*how can they not have crushed self-esteems due to everyday pressure?* We really have to ask and seek answers to this question!

Can we teach all children to flourish and have a positive outlook on life?

Can we truly love ourselves, and accept all of our flaws?

If we fully accepted them, would we see them as flaws?

This world needs more love so desperately. Through the eyes of an adoptee, this is a desperation I know. But the love I have felt and experienced gives me hope that one day love will reign and people will be accepted exactly for who they are.

CHAPTER 11

The Emotional Journey of Adoption

Before we get to the heart of an adoptee's emotions, I have to offer a disclaimer: I am not an adoption expert and all opinions contained in this chapter come through my personal experiences only.

Before I graduated from college, I completed a research paper for my family class on the subject of adoption. It involved months of researching, conducting personal surveys and compiling the results with the purpose of understanding the emotions associated with adoption. It was based on my own emotions and those of others expressed in the research. There is a widespread lack of understanding the emotions that an adopted person has, and being that my goal is to help as many people I can with this book, it makes sense to share my research in depth. I found the most common emotions summed up in the following words often used (and situations referred to) by adoptees: *lost, abandonment, hopelessness, anger, guilt, rejection, fantasy, death of a parent, not being acknowledged by other family members, control, helplessness, internalized emotions, cumulative grief, sadness, loss of culture, transracial adoption,* and *trust.*

The following interpretation of these words is my perspective; I am not speaking on others' behalf. Their emotions are theirs and theirs alone; I honor that one-hundred percent! This list is not a reflection on my adoptive family; these feelings are separate from them. My research has had the full support of my family, who understands the need for me to find myself.

Lost. To me, being lost means that I don't fit in anywhere, that I have no place in this world, and that my whole life was decided without my consent. Even if the decision makers' intentions were pure, it doesn't mean that I don't feel lost. *Where do I belong and where is my home? Whom do I belong to and with whom am I connected? Who is my family? Are the biological connections that were lost to me ever rectified? Where are the lost family members that knew of my existence? Where are the people who were involved in my life? Am I a lost soul belonging nowhere? Are lost souls suspended in time? How is it that my heart feels that way? Are others as lost as I feel?* Being lost emotionally is very different than being lost physically. We can find our way back with a GPS when we are lost physically. I have not found an emotional GPS.

I have often felt that I am lost in a maze in which, wherever I turn, I hit a road block, and there is no way out. It's as if I'm at the mercy of the maze itself to find the way out, with no guidance at all. It's a natural maze consisting of high bushes, and they tower above me. It's dark and foggy and it feels damp, like a fall day after a rain. All I have is a broken candle with no lighter, so I wander with no light to guide my way. I turn around at every dead end, and try to feel my way out maze, but the walls keep closing in. What happens next is that the turns keep spinning and I hit a wall, then try to go through the wall without success. Where is the key to unlock the door at the end of the maze? Who holds the key to let me out?

Abandonment. For anyone who has ever been abandoned or given up, no matter at what age, this word can linger and affect their life choices. People who have been abandoned need compassion. Please don't look down on them.

What causes someone to abandon another human being, let alone a baby? Does an abandoned child play out the issue their whole life? Do they look for mothers or fathers in other people? Do they enter into bad relationships because of it? Is it the reason why they never feel truly whole? Is the thought of being abandoned so embedded in the brain that they are not able to get past it? I get infuriated when we people say things like "just get over being adopted" or "you have a cherished and privileged life, what do you possibly have to be angry about?" Easily said by people who have not walked a mile in my shoes.

Hopelessness. Hope is something that humans hold onto—it is why we pray for healing. It inspires us to believe things will get better, no matter how dark it gets. We need to envision the light and feel that *something* is going to lift us again—hope gives us that.

Is hope the answer? Or does it cause a false sense of security? Hopelessness, in my experience as an adopted person, creeps in when we lose our belief in hope. Let me explain that. I have hopes and dreams of finding biological connections. That's what drives me to keep searching, to perhaps find at least one family member alive. Hope drives me, no matter if people say there is no chance in hell; I am going to find at least one family member alive.

Many people ask me, "What is it like to search for your biological ancestors?"

I respond, "It's. like looking for a needle in a haystack."

Some people go on from there. "What if they don't want to be found?" or "what if they don't want you at all?"

"This is a risk," I tell them. I have two different girlfriends who were adopted and they each found their biological family, yet neither of their experiences was good. They wish they had never met them. One friend is worse off now and wishes she didn't know her birth mother at all. All the issues she had were escalated to a whole other level; she had learned the truth of her story and the truth was beyond devastating to her. She and my other friend have warned me that the fantasy of what my biological family is and what is truly the reality can be harsh to stomach.

My heart has known the depths of hopelessness, but I still have hope. Hopelessness would prevent me from doing a lot of things, but giving up this search is not an option for me.

Anger. In the Kübler-Ross model, the stages of grief are: *Denial, Anger, Bargaining, depression and acceptance.* In adoptees, anger manifests itself in very different ways. Often it is internalized.

In fact, I am certain that I have not dealt with all of my anger, given my non-confrontational personality. But I strive to deal with it in healthy ways. For example, when I become aware of it through writing, I process it on the page until it is no longer internalized, and do not take it out on people.

Anger may also manifest as jealousy of the biological children within the family. Are all adoptive children jealous of the biological children? Or is it simply sibling rivalry? Can anger have to do with birth order within a family? I am the youngest and the only daughter. Again, I was not treated any differently because I was adopted, yet I have not been immune to angry feelings common among adoptees.

Guilt. Guilt is a word that carries way too much power. I know it intimately, due to the issues and circumstances surrounding my birth mother's death and my adoption. Yes, it stops us from making bad decisions. But it is also a tremendous weight. Do we ever truly want to do something out of guilt? Can't we just do something for people simply because we love them and because we want to?

How do we let go of guilt? Even if we had nothing to do with a situation. One time, responsibility was placed on me for a situation concerning my adoption over which I *knew* I had no control and I still felt an astronomical proportions of guilt. It took me two years to process it internally and then finally talk about it with trusted loved ones. Sometimes I can't let go of things and I have to accept that. In the same breath, I pray for resolution of the situation, and that I may contribute to it in the best way I can. Being that I was a people pleaser until about fifteen years ago, I have learned to not be driven by guilt or what others will think of me and my actions. Guilt is learned and then it is unlearned, as it has been in my experience by aiming to do everything out of pure love and good intentions.

Rejection. Acceptance is something most humans strive for, so much that our entire culture is built around it. Conventional success in school and work basically depends on being accepted by your peers and fitting it. *Are you accepted into the clique? Are you accepted by your co-workers? Do you fit in within your community?*

I don't know anyone who has not experienced some form of rejection. No matter the reason, it doesn't make rejection less painful. But for someone to reject a child at such an early stage in life definitely lays a foundation that affects self-worth. The fear of rejection could be a fear many of us share. It is the reason why many of us only share our true selves with people who love us unconditionally. Because we know that will be accepted, without any strings attached. Either way rejection does not feel good. It causes us to internally to wonder, *why?* I have been wondering my whole life if something I did led me to be rejected at such an early age.

Fantasy. Why do people squash other people's dreams and hopes? Nothing infuriates me more than when I share a dream with someone and they say, "You'll never be able to achieve that." When it comes to adoptees, we tend to fantasize about our birth parents a lot. I have never met an adopted person who hasn't had that experience, not to say there couldn't be some. But just because I fantasize about my birth parents, it doesn't mean that I love my parents who adopted me any less. One thing has nothing to do with the other. It doesn't make me an ungrateful daughter, for wanting me to know my biological roots.

Fantasizing about a birth mother and father seems normal to me. *Is it because of the primal drive? Or is it the feelings of rejection that we need to resolve?* The chance to ask them if I did something that led to being given up—that is one of the dreams in my heart. Maybe knowing the answer would help to heal my self-esteem.

Death of a Parent. *Is mourning someone you never knew possible?* I feel in my heart it is. I have a friend who finally located her birth father; unfortunately he had died the same week that she found him. She was able to attend his funeral, and as painful as it was, it gave her a small connection to him. She got to mourn the loss. She has warned me about the possibility that the same thing could happen to me.

What happens if someone searches their whole life and then finds this out? Are humans mentally prepared for that possibility? I can honestly say, "I have no idea." I have not figured out the right way to mourn my birth mother. Not sure if I ever will. It deeply pains me that I don't know her name. When I am in India, I drive by cemeteries and wonder if she's buried in one of them. What if there was no body and she was just cremated? Here is a woman who gave her life for me, and I don't even know her name? How is that possible?

Losing a parent is one of the worst things people can go through. I have seen it a lot. How do you mourn the people who raised you and helped to shape your life? You are who you are because of them.

Just because I didn't meet my birthmother doesn't meant that I don't love her and have this dream of who she was, and what she looked like. *Did I have her eyes? Do I have her nose? Am I a carbon copy of her? Would she be proud of me? Am I the person that she hoped I would be? Is she angry at me because I caused her death? Could my grandparents ever forgive me for that, that they lost a daughter, and never got their granddaughter? Was she dreaming of me when she was pregnant, in the hope of us being together forever? Did she sing to me? Did we dance together? Did we skip and play while I was in her belly? Did she talk to me? Was her voice memorized in my head? Where was her voice? Did she get to hold me the two days before she passed? Why don't I have a memory of her? Why does it feel like there is a hole inside of me that will never close? Do I just have to accept that fact? Do I have to live in a cloud of confusion and unanswered questions?*

To the people who have lost a parent, my heart goes out to you. And to the people who are out there who are looking for their biological parents, I wish you the best in your search. Don't let someone keep you from having dreams. Our dreams are our dreams, and no one can tell you any differently.

Not being acknowledged by any other family members. I have heard stories where an adoptee finds extended biological family and they were told that didn't know they existed, because they were never told about them. The question for the adoptee becomes "why weren't they told about me?"

Why are there so many secrets when it comes to adoption? What is there to hide? If it is hidden that a person is adopted, it risks bringing a whole other layer of shame on to the adoptee. Adoptees are *not* dirty little secrets. Secrets always have a way of getting out. I truly feel bad for people whose parents lied to them and didn't tell them they were adopted until later in life.

Control. I would love to know the answer to this question: *how in the world are adoptees supposed to have control?* I'm not talking about being out of control. I am talking about having a choice in decisions that affect one's life. I had zero control as an infant. This was challenging to accept but now makes complete sense to me. Perhaps it explains why control issues are not one of my defining characteristics. Having no choice in matters of my adoption, a certain "let it go, let it be" attitude is part of my personality.

Control is going to be controversial word. What baby has control of their lives? Babies are at the mercy of their parents, whether you are a biological child or an adoptee. But still it seems to me that the feeling of having no control explains a lot. I went through a period of not feeling in control of my life, where I was lost and trying to find myself. Isn't that what the twenties are all about? I think our twenties are about making mistakes, our thirties are about getting it together and our forties are about analyzing it all. Why did we do what we did? Even though everything we have done has shaped us as human beings, it doesn't mean we understand all of our actions. *Will we ever fully understand why we do the things that we do?*

Control seems to exist on a continuum. Are there things in this world that are out of our control? Yes, absolutely. Do we have to be in control of everything? Probably not. Sometimes we need to let our lives unfold naturally.

Helplessness. Wow, this is a word that radiates through my soul. Why? It's simple: I have felt helpless in a lot of life situations. I felt helpless as a baby. I felt helpless in miscarrying a baby, and I felt helpless with the adoption falling apart. I had no control over the fact that I needed surgeries. I felt helpless in those times and with anything that had to do with my body. It makes sense that this word would resonate with adoptees, as we've had little to no input into so many life-altering decisions made on our behalf.

Internalizing Emotions. I am a perfect example of someone who internalizes emotions. Even though I am a deeply emotional person, it has taken me years to truly share my emotions with people. I'm not clear why that is, but I have some ideas. It could be rooted in uncertainty that my feelings would be accepted. It also could be that I grew up in a very vocal family, and didn't feel my voice would be heard. This is not their doing; we are wired differently.

It is common knowledge that it is healthier to get one's emotions out. As I wrote this book, I wore my emotions on my sleeve—not a normal state of mind for me. It was an effort to process everything and let it flow, while accepting all of the emotions that surfaced.

It can't be healthy for the body to hold onto emotions. I admire the people who just speak their minds and express their emotions the minute they rise inside of them. I am not referring to people who have zero control of their emotions. I do believe that we need a filter and pray that people think before they speak.

Cumulative Grief. Cumulative grief is experienced in the wake of multiple losses. It can also be interpreted as grief overload. This is something we all have seen, where people have experienced way too much grief in their lives. Or they have had grief upon grief. In other words, have they had time to recover from one grief before another grief occurs? It has been explained to me that unless we deal with all the grief that comes our way, it will stick around until we deal with it.

Being someone who has experienced grief overload, I get it. Because I haven't fully dealt with my grief, it has its ways of rearing its head at the most inopportune times. If adoptees hold on to grief, will it shape the way we function throughout our lives? Are we subject to the feeling of primal loss, the loss of our biological parents, throughout our whole lives? It seems like it would put us back in the maze that I talked about in the discussion of feeling "lost."

Do we have control over grief? Maybe we are not supposed to have control over it, and it just controls us? Is it a lost battle, which we will not win? Are adoptees then grieving their whole lives?

Sadness. Sadness is something that comes with the territory of being adopted. Sadness over the loss of family. Sadness over the loss of country and culture. Sadness over questions of identity. Sadness of the reality that one might never find their biological family members. Sadness over the possibility that the people you are searching for might have passed away. Sadness about not belonging anywhere.

This sadness that can be carried with an adoptee for their whole life. What to do with the sadness? Where does it go? Does it ever truly go away? Mine comes and goes. Ninety-five percent of the time, I am a truly happy, joyful person. But there are moments when sadness occurs and I am learning to feel my way through the process. Writing this book has torn open my heart. It has felt as though a precious crystal has shattered and I've been struggling to slowly find every piece and glue it all back together.

As an adoptee are you sentenced to a life of sadness? Or are there options for us? I have been told that I will be healthier for writing this book, after finding my way out of the labyrinth of emotions. The problem is that sadness radiates throughout the body, where my cells are shaking, and where I can feel them vibrating. It's a visceral experience that can be all consuming. We know there are underlying causes. The question then is how to lift the dark cloud around the head to bring the sunshine back into life.

Loss of Culture. This is a big one for me and other adoptees who have experienced the same feelings. I can only share my experience on this topic. I was born in one culture and country and was sent to America, where I was given another culture and religion and identity. International adoption adds a whole other layer to adoptees. Whether adopted within the States or out of the States, adoptees face many different emotions related to geographical changes and family culture changes. This explains my fascination with the field of Cultural Psychology.

Being adopted, I lost my birth nation, my religion (although I am not sure what that religion I was born into), and my language, the one I heard spoken during the nine months inside my mother's womb. My parents encouraged me to explore my culture, but I wasn't open to it until much later in life. It had to do with the fact that I felt I didn't fit in anywhere culturally. I didn't have Indian friends growing up, nor did I explore other religions that I might have been connected to in India. America is a melting pot and my question was *where do I fit in, in that melting pot?*

I didn't truly understand the ramifications of cultural loss until I was older and went back to India for the first time. It's about having a connection to your biological culture from which you came from. It's about being able to identify with your culture. There is no one to blame in this scenario. It's the way international adoption is, or was my experience. I am connected to Indian friends now. I am more connected to my culture than I have ever been, and that truly fills my heart. I love America and India. My love for one country doesn't diminish the love for another country. Let me be crystal clear on that.

I was given a new wonderful country and a new religion. I was given a *new identity!* I was asked to assimilate into a new country and a new family. Then be assimilated into a new religion. The core of me was wiped away and I was to begin again. I was Indian woman, who became an Indian Jewish woman. Again, *not easy* to be that in America. My parents did their absolute best for me to fit in within the family culture, which I totally did; but here I am talking about outside the family.

I believe there should be some kind of form adoptees fill out when they are a little older and can make their own decisions. Let me give you an example what I think should be on the form:

1. What culture do you want to be part of?

2. What religion do you want to be part of?

3. Do you want to study the language of your heritage?

4. Do you want to learn to cook the food of culture?

5. Do you want to make your own choices?

6. What would help you to assimilate better?

7. Are we helping you to assimilate?

8. What are your needs and wants?

Will this list help others to understand adoptees better? I hope so. I do believe that these choices should be given to the adoptee. I have wondered, *Why is it that adoptees are told to assimilate, and change everything that we have known? Why is that OK? Where is the compassion? Why do we have to give up everything we have known? Why can't we choose for ourselves?* Please put the choice of future decisions in the adoptees hands. That's all I ask, on behalf of my adopted brother and sisters in every culture.

Culturally I have struggled with the lack of the presence of my birth culture in my life. Learning more about it really has made my heart fuller. I am a proud Indian American—I can't state that enough!!—and there is a part of me that was not healed until I went back to my birth country. When did it happen? Let me try to paint a picture for you.

It was on the steps, when I exited the airport and my feet touched down in India for the first time in over thirty years.

It was the hearing the sounds of India: the motorcycles whirling, the sounds of wildlife everywhere, the voices of multiple languages, the busy markets and the sound of fast-paced-moving energy everywhere.

It was seeing my first Indian sunrise. It was the smell of curry cooking and chai tea simmering. It was the vision of monkeys and cows walking around me. It was the colors—*amethyst, cerulean, cobalt, fuchsia, scarlet, saffron, gold, lime and silver*—that lit up my eyes. India affects all the senses. It is a visceral experience for mind, body and soul.

Despite how at home I felt, I had a lot of cultural learning to do the first time I visited India. People corrected me in polite ways. One example was on what to wear. I wear tank tops in the United States but I do not wear them in India. I change my clothing style out of the level of respect I have for the India's cultures and customs. Cultural loss is a real phenomenon, yet I believe it can be healed in time with awareness and genuine willingness to explore our roots.

Trust. Trust is a big one. If an adoptee can't trust people as they get older, is it because they were adopted? If one's initial relationships (meaning before adoption) were severed due to circumstances not in their control, does this affect trust later on?

If people weren't there for them as a baby, or they were abandoned as a baby, it makes complete sense that they would have trust issues. I am a prime example. It takes a lot for me to trust someone one-hundred percent. If I give you my trust and you break it, I will probably not be so forgiving of that. Why? Because it took me a long time to trust you in the first place, and then you broke it. I'm sure this is pretty typical for a lot of people, adopted or not. One can't blame everything on adoption. Trust issues affect everyone. Here I am only applying it to an adoptee's experience. I can't speak for all adoptees; I can only share my personal experiences with trust.

Transracial Adoption. With so many mixed families now, I do not quite understand why there is still a stigma associated with it? People still ask me and mom, what is the relationship? *Am I her caregiver? Am I her nurse? Basically, what service am I providing her?* It blows my mind that people make the assumption, and it's not OK. I don't get it; I don't go up to people and straight out ask them about their families or situations? What gives people the right?

Our extended family is built on adoption, so for us it's completely normal. I remember my mother, aunt, and adopted cousin were on one of our mother-daughter trips, years ago. We were checking into a *very* nice hotel and it was obvious that the attendant working the desk was confused. He went on to ask, "Who belongs to whom?" WTF? What you mean? We belong to each other!! We are a family no matter what our race is?

Look, I get it—I'm never going to change racism in this country on my own. It does not mean that I have to accept it. My husband and I last fall, walked into a super common restaurant. It was amazing how quiet it got and how people just stared at us; we left because we felt unsafe. Just because I am Indian and he's white, you could almost hear a pin drop. Is it 2018? Or have we stepped back in time?

It shouldn't matter whether families are mixed. Doesn't it matter more that a child has a home? That the child has a family that loves for them and cares for them, versus what the options could be? If people stopped judging others for what people do choose to live with their lives, this world might become a better place.

For the people who don't support transracial adoptions, I believe they should question why they feel that way. If a child is adopted by a loving, supportive family, isn't that all that matters? Yes, there will be cultural loss to deal with but that can be healed. If everyone in the world had even an ounce of compassion and understanding, it would make a beautiful difference.

This chapter has focused on the emotions that surround adoption through, my eyes. My hope in sharing all the emotions that I have encountered, is that it will help people who are adopted to not feel so alone, and to help people have a better understanding of adopted people.

Beyond this list of adoptees' emotions and common situations, there are many more feelings and scenarios that adoptees experience. I have done my best to give you a small insight into what some adoptees experience—and now all I ask is for compassion for my adopted brothers and sisters across the world.

CHAPTER 12

My Hope for the World

I magine a painter who does not paint by number. Instead, on a blank canvas, she allows the paintbrush to unleash her soul. Writing this book has been like that: the keyboard has been my paint brush, and it has set my soul free. A major of the healing has been the buried questions that it brought to the surface, questions I share here in this chapter. They come from the voice of my heart. Finding my voice has gifted me hope for the world—and I am now using my voice to express that hope and an ideal vision for the future.

What is the true meaning of life? Is everyone's meaning different from others meanings? Is our life plan laid out, or is it a series of events? Are we just playing out roles given to us? Or do we have a say in our life? Do events truly shape us? Is the universe changing our plans? Is there something bigger than all of us? Are human beings able to acknowledge that it might be out of their control?

Life is full of surprises. It is never a straight line; it weaves and moves in a fluid motion. I have learned that we can have the *greatest* plans laid out for us, and then it all unfolds differently. Now, what do we do with it? Do we bury our heads in the sand, or do we move forward and dig our way out? Everyone handles change differently; certain coping mechanisms that work for one person will not necessarily work for another. We are not all wired the same, and this is a good thing, too.

I don't want to be the same as someone else. And in times of change and transformation, I don't set high expectations for when I am supposed to feel better. Time is what it is and no one can set an alarm clock for when pain and grief should end. Admittedly I have issues with people saying, "You should be over it by now." What difference does it make if I heal on my own time schedule?

I tell them, "Just let me be, and I'll find my way."

Meanwhile, my inner voice speaks loud and clear within me. *I don't need your input on how I should heal myself. Have you been though what I have? I ask. And for that matter, since I have not been through what you have been through, I will not offer unsolicited advice. What I will offer is empathy and compassion. I will listen to you.*

My Hope for the World

There is so much that I would love to see this world accomplish: the end to poverty, hunger, wars, abuse on every level, and disease. Having witnessed these, I wish I could wave a want to fix all of it. I do not have first-hand experience with war, but some of my family members have. Shower a soldier with love and it could never be enough, given the sacrifices they have made for our country. How many of us have sacrificed for our country or would?

Once in a while of I find myself in a grocery checkout line next to a soldier, and I'll buy their groceries for them. It's just a small way to thank them for all their service. I envision my brother-in-law who has served for a long time, and has done a lot of tours overseas, and wish someone will do the same for him.

What if we all paid it forward? Would we live in a world of peace and harmony? What if there weren't abandoned children roaming the streets of the world? What if all women in the world have equal rights? Can everything that I dream about for this world really come to fruition?

People often invite me to speak on diversity awareness, or how to run a small business, or women empowerment issues; and in my talks, I always project my highest vision for the world, no matter how far-fetched it seems. In one talk I had given a few years ago, the audience was full of women and men ages eighteen and older. It was one of those talks where I wondered, *Am I reaching anyone?*

Typically I receive feedback from the event coordinator afterward, but I still never know if I impacted someone's life. About three years following this particular speech, a young woman approached me in the store and said she remembered me from the speech I had given. She went on to say that I had deeply moved her and she could still hear my words. Now I was the one who was moved.

Just about to give another speech at a college, I was feeling the anxiety that I get before I give a speech, wondering if I could do it. Would the speech impact college students?

Thank goodness for this random act of kindness, this young woman's courage to approach a stranger and share from her heart. Hearing her words gave me the courage to continue to speak. It inspired me, as it affirmed that I was helping people, which was one of my original goals. I believe that moment was karmic. Because I needed the courage for the next talk, I deeply appreciated our encounter that day.

As for the writing of this book, it has deeply impacted me on many levels. It tore me up emotionally to revisit old wounds and pain. On days it felt as if my heart were being unraveled by many small threads, and that I was transported, as if by time machine, back to the exact moment where the sad events were happening all over again. It's great and wonderful when the memories are happy—we love to revisit those! But the traumatic ones are a different story, literally.

At times the memories appeared to hinder all the progress I had worked so hard for in my life. Despite my forward movement, the memories had a tendency to pull me back. On some days it felt as if I were running as fast as I could, against the strongest wind possible and the wind current was so strong, that I couldn't even imagine advancing one step in the right direction. But if my revelations can help to ease another person's pain, then I know it will all be worth it in the end.

Is the real purpose of our lives to help others? Or is it to help ourselves? I hope it is to help others. I hope that humanity rises up and makes the world a better place. That we pitch in and give of ourselves in any way that we can. Whether it is our time, talents or money we share, we can make this world a better place—a place that feels like home.

CHAPTER 13

I Remember Home

In 2015, I was traveling in India and taking photos all over. I went to visit a leper colony (yes leprosy is still very much happening). Like the United States, India is broken into states. I was in the state of Tamil Nadu, and close to the city of Kasam, where I was born. There I met a woman who would forever change me. The executive director was showing me around as a volunteer photographer there to help a nonprofit organization in need of publicity and marketing support. Let me be clear, I was not there to photograph without humility. I was there to take photos to create an awareness that leprosy was still going on and to leave a donation, to help the organization care for people with leprosy.

I came across an elderly woman who was sitting cross-legged in a beautiful orange sari, and I'm not lying, when I tell you, she had the most beautiful smile I had ever seen in my life. There was something about her, and I was completely drawn to her.

I sat on the ground and introduced myself to her. The director translated for me our conversations. I asked about her story. In summary, she is a woman who is blind and deaf and has leprosy. I was shocked and my heart broke for her. I took many photos of her, with her permission. She just kept smiling, and she rubbed my cheeks and hugged me.

I had to ask, "What does she have to be happy about?" Blindness, deafness and leprosy. The director looked me in the eye and said, "She was homeless, and we took her in, and now she has a home, and she is very grateful for that."

Wow! There she was, somewhere in the middle of this great big world. I had the honor of meeting her, and *I got my lesson of happiness, and gratitude from her.*

Meeting her reaffirmed the fact that *there is so much to be happy about and grateful for.*

I know I met her for a reason—more than just to photograph her, to write about her, and to end this book with her message. Whenever I think of her, I feel her happiness for simply being alive. She has taught me humility and the true worth of seeing the sunshine through the clouds. I thank her and can't wait to visit her again. In the meantime, I love to share her story and carry her with me. This way wherever I may go, my heart swells with the same gratitude and I remember home.

In Conclusion

Right now, my heart is bursting with ideas I've wanted to write about in this conclusion. It is always said that, in a conclusion, the writer should return to the purpose stated in the introduction and review what goals have been in writing the book. But this is not a scholarly paper. Been there, done that. I'd like to end this more like a symphony, with thoughts that take the ideas in this book to the next higher octave.

As I wrote this book, the 2017 events of Charlottesville, Virginia, were unfolding. I was sick to my core watching what happened, as I'm sure you reading this book share this sentiment. *Was this really happening in the country I call home?* I have met people who think racism is dead in this country. *How is that possible?* It saddens me because I truly fear for my safety when I walk out my door.

This is not OK.

During the Charlottesville tragedy, I was invited to be the keynote speaker at public event to promote peace and love. Yet I truly felt that given the climate in the U.S., it would not be safe for me. I knew they would understand, and I fully supported them in planning the event, but did not speak publicly, reflecting a sad state of affairs.

When people ask me if we have advanced in this country, my answer is no. Then I wonder, *What were the Civil Rights about? Where is the forward progression in this country? Why are we moving back? What is it going to take for this amazing country to realize hate is never the answer for anything? What does hate accomplish?* There should never a be reason to hate someone for their skin color, religion, or sexual preferences. There is no place for this in any place people call home.

One reason why I give talks is to help dispel stereotypes people have about certain races, religions and gender. While I teach about Judaism, and being Indian, and being a woman, I am also an example of every person who embraces their heritage and find that people connect with me on that level, no matter their religion, race or gender. I'm very open and answer all the questions that people ask me. This is how to combat hate, through education. By creating a discussion where people can ask and answer questions in an open forum in which people feel safe to engage. I congratulate all who are creating these public discussions.

I will continue to pray for this world. Will my prayers work? *Would love be enough for this country? What if we changed our views, but didn't give up our principles?* I'm not talking about accepting people's hate or prejudices—I'm talking about how there has to be another way, for us to resolve conflicts, to remain loyal to our beliefs, and to avoid violence at any cost. *Are my goals for this world are completely unrealistic?* A girl can still dream.

For that matter, am I supposed to know? Or am I supposed to just keep dreaming? Is enlightenment possible? Are all of our dreams attainable or are they just suspended in the universe as the stars are? If dreams are unattainable then why do we have them? Even if they are unattainable, do they help motivate us to reach our goals?

Seeing the Sunshine Through the Clouds

I have been told that I see life through rose-colored glasses, that my daydreams are too big, that my head is up in the clouds. I have decided that my head in the clouds is OK! Like many, I have suffered too much. So what if I want to see this world as a world of butterflies and roses? It brings me joy and happiness.

I have photographed the worst of this world. I have seen tragic things most people have not. My saving grace is that *I still try to see the good things in life.* I am sure it is part of my survival mechanism.

So for a moment, let's talk about the wonderful things in this world: *sunrises, the smell of roses, the sounds of laughter, the sight of a loved one, the taste of a crème brûlée, the smell of coffee rising in the air, the warmth of a fireplace on a winters day, the arrival of spring, and the ocean waves crashing against the shoreline, the sight of a sunflower farm, the warmth of our dogs kisses, the smell of Thanksgiving cooking, and being awestruck of piece of art that is so moving, it captivates our souls.*

All of this—and there are still more things to be grateful for. I want to acknowledge all of it. Because while there is sadness in this world, there is plenty of joy. There are good people out there trying their best to help others. There is compassion and love and kindness and harmony in life as well. Part of why I know this is that these qualities have arisen in my heart, as a desire to help others by sharing my experience. This is how I will serve for the rest of my days.

What I Wish I Knew Sooner about the Topics in this Book
Although this book encapsulates my story, my goal in writing it is to help others. Whether the experiences were good or bad, I wanted to share what I have learned from all of it. So here are some things, which I wish I knew and would have been better for, in the areas of adoption, loss of motherhood, and rediscovering home.

Adoption:
20 Tips for Finding Your Way Through Adoption

As I have stated, I am no expert in this field, just someone who has seen adoption from many different angles. Here are list of things that I wish I would have known about when attempting to adopt a child. In sharing this list, I pray that no other couple out there will experience what my husband and I did. I was naïve in thinking that our adoption agency had our best interests at heart; not at all was that the truth. For many reasons, I do not disclose the name of the agency. Yet I have spoken to an adoption expert with twenty years of experience in the field and she is clear that the way our case was handled was completely wrong on multiple levels. I do know there are wonderful agencies out there. If it weren't for adoption, a lot of people would not have children, and a lot of kids would not have homes. Let me say this again, I was a person who was adopted, and I'm grateful for that experience and for my family. I question all the time, what my life would be like if I hadn't been. Adoption through my eyes is a 360-degree experience.

Here are items to note when adopting a child and raising them:

1. Make sure that both biological parents have surrendered their rights.

2. Are people telling the truth? Hopefully you can find that out.

3. Is there a supportive system in place for the adoptive parents? There was none for us. When we arrived at a hospital, no one was there to meet us. We did everything through email and the phone. Please don't make the same mistake. Find out beforehand who will be there to help you.

4. Have a lawyer on your side.

5. Have a social worker on your side.

6. Document everything.

7. Keep every receipt while you travel. There are tax credits for adoption. There are tax credits for failed adoptions as well.

8. Have a good accountant who is familiar with handling adoptions.

9. Consider preparing the child's room after the adoption is successful. This is a personal choice for everyone, yet I truly wish I hadn't done the nursery before. That was so hard to come home to. Everyone will decide what is best for them, but believe me when I say that I wish I hadn't.

10. Ask for the any and all medical information you can get on the birth family.

11. Learn about your child's culture and aim to provide it to them.

12. Just because a child wants to search out their roots, it doesn't mean that they don't love you. (I hear this concern a lot from adoptees and adopted parents). Love is fluid and grows exponentially.

13. Have compassion and drop the expectation that your adoptive child is going to be like you, just because you are raising them. Please do some research on this. There is a lot of good reading on nature versus nurture.

14. Please *don't refer* to your child as "the adopted child." If my parents had done that, which *they didn't,* I would have felt like an outsider completely. I'm their daughter. Period. The end.

15. Support adopted kids in processing their emotions, especially the ones listed in Chapter 11.

16. Let your child connect with other adoptees. It helps me a lot when I speak with other people who have been adopted, and learn that they experience many of the same emotions that I have.

17. A support system is crucial. Make sure your child has access to people who they love and trust. I have been lucky in this sense, given the friends and family who have been there for me. As I am still reaching my own roots, it's not always good what I find out, so I rely on them for love and support. I have realized that I am too emotionally tied into the situation, and I need the outside advice from others who can speak to me logically. I need to bounce ideas around with them.

18. Question everything and encourage your child to do the same. I have become more skeptical as I research my roots and that may not be a bad thing. I'm often afraid to provide real, truthful information about my past when I don't understand the reason for being asked certain questions. Always make sure the reason for sharing personal information is clearly defined and the situation is safe before doing so.

19. Keep your eyes open. I failed in that sense. My heart had wanted a child so badly that I didn't see all the red flags that were more apparent in hindsight. My biological need to have a child superseded everything else. I wish I didn't use my heart to cloud my judgment as much as I did.

20. Even though I'm a glass-half-full kind of woman, I have learned that people's true intentions are not always in your best interest. We have to take care of ourselves and our needs, and protect ourselves. Just be smart, and don't give people the power to dictate how you should be living your life.

My hope in sharing this this list is for people who are adopting to have a wonderful experience. In no way is this list meant to scare people about adoption. I know there are a lot of successful adoptions out there and that is all I wish for people.

Loss of Motherhood:
6 Tips for Finding Your Way Through Miscarriage, Surgery or Failed Adoption

If you find yourself in this deeply emotional situation, here are some ideas that might be helpful in finding your way through it.

1. Are their support groups available in your area? Support is crucial when you miscarry or lose the dream of being a mother in some other way. It is a huge help to speak with others who have been through it. My support system was crucial to healing.

2. Could planting a tree help you? Can you create a memorial service to help bring healing to you and your husband or partner?

3. Do you have an outlet for your emotions? Are they healthy outlets? Is there something creative that you could do for your grief? Trust me when I say that I

wish I would have handled all my grief very differently. I tucked it down and it kept coming up. Please don't make the same mistake I did. Feel your grief as it rises. I understand that everyone deals with grief differently. I refer you back to Chapter 4 if you feel drawn to contemplate it further.

4. Be a patient advocate.

5. People will give you a lot of advice. Unfortunately, unless they have been through it, it is hard to hear their words. They mean well.

6. Pursuing an art was helpful for me too. It seemed to help soothe unconscious emotions, which I was not dealing with.

To the women and couples who have lost a baby, I understand and will keep you in my thoughts and prayers. If there are things that helped you, please share them with the people who need to hear about them. I have talked to so many women and couples who just felt alone, and there is no need to go through this alone.

Rediscovering Home:
9 Tips for Finding Your Way Through Life

The main theme of this book is how to find a new way *when life changes your plans.* This list is a summary of key things that help me along my journey, and I hope it helps others as well.

1. **Have a strong, healthy support system**. I wholeheartedly believe that if you surround yourself with *healthy* people, you will be healthier for it. When I look back at time periods when I was with unhealthy people, I can see how it all deeply affected me. Make healthy choices when it comes to relationships. You'll be better for it.

2. **Expect the unexpected**. That is pretty much my new mantra. I have had my life plans laid out before me, and you can see how that all worked out. Not so much. So I have learned to go with the flow more. Life will unfold in the way that it does.

3. **Embrace therapy**. Don't be so quick not to ask for help when you need it. I am forever grateful to the therapists who helped me through all of it. You are not a weak person for wanting therapy. Isn't there a point where we can only handle so much, and it's OK to get help? Of course there is.

4. **Exercise**. Moving my body is always a huge help for me. Walking with my dogs for years helped me to clear my mind and gain perspective. Tread off the beaten path and find your place of solitude. My sacred place is by a waterfall, as that is the first place where I ever felt my heart start to heal.

5. **Discover your passion and live it.** I started my photography business shortly after the adoption fell through. Finding my passion is what truly saved my life. I remain ever grateful to my cousin, who said, "What do you love to do? And why are you not doing it?" His words were powerful. If you are not doing what you love, and you want to, go for it! Everyone has something that they are passionate about, but for one reason or another, many people don't live their passion. If we listened to our souls more, would we be happier? In my experience, the answer is *yes!* Passion can guide us on the right path. It has been crucial for me, in all of my healing processes.

6. **Don't apologize for who you are.** This I have learned as I have gotten older. To stop caring about what others think of me has freed me up to be the true me. It has freed up my mind to concentrate on what truly matters in my life. It has opened a new path where I no longer live in fear of people's judgments and criticisms. I spent too much time in my life caring, as in high school when I wanted so badly to fit in. Now I wish I could have all that time back. I love people for who they are and don't ask them to change. I love them unconditionally and I love myself in this same way by not apologizing for who I am.

7. **Make understanding a goal.** I realized that there has to come a time when we try to understand why things happen the way they do. How did this help me to find a new path? It was through understanding that I learned to let go of some anger. I'm still angry about certain things, but the load has lessened over the years and that is helping me to heal. I also have learned to let go of things that were not all my fault, and to accept that there were other things in the universe that were planned for me. Understanding has helped me to have more compassion for others.

8. **Appreciate the idea of karma.** Karma is the reason why I do everything—I will always and forever treat people the way I want to be treated. I will put the

good I can into this world. Will the universe reward me for good deeds? I don't know and I don't care, because I will continue to good things for others, because we all should. I know a lot of my life plan is based on karma, because it guides me. Try a path of giving and not taking and see what happens? Does your life plan change?

9. **Slow down.** I would say that I have two speeds: 150% and 0. I'm either moving at a fast pace, or I am able to shut down completely. This dichotomy of fast versus slow works for me, but slowing down is what has allowed me to really treasure moments with other human beings. Whether it's a cup of coffee with a friend, or a long, lazy lunch with family, these simple moments are gifts. I try to not to rush the times that mean the most to me. Be in the moment, and hold on to it in your heart.

My intention, for this book and in life is to help as many people as I can. I hope that people realize that in my sharing all that I have shared in this book, none of it was easy for me. These pages reveal the most I have ever shared in my whole life! But the fire inside of me, of wanting to help others, was lit up every day.

Someone recently said to me that she could never write a book or submit it to a publisher for fear of rejection. She asked me, "How are you doing it?"

I said, "I would rather try. I don't want to have one more regret in my life." I explained I'm so driven in wanting to help others, that whatever becomes of the book, I am OK with it.

I had to write this book not only for others but also for myself. As I explained many times, writing this book pulled open my heart and ripped into many pieces. If all my heartaches *help others pain to heal,* then it will all be worth it. No one should feel alone in this world. I hope my words will make someone *feel less alone* when they are going through many of the experiences that I have shared in this book.

All that being said, I realized what I have written in this will probably resonate more with people who have been through common experiences that I have shared. Or with people who have friends or family members who have gone through many of the experiences. *Does all of life have to be so easy, or are the struggles we go through help us to be better people? What is the answer to that?* Maybe we will never know. That might be something that I just have to accept, the unknowing in life.

For me, life is no longer a laid out plan. It is has taught me to be more fluid and face anything that comes my way. That in itself is a lesson. I am more adaptable to situations when they arise. I know that life takes planning, but sometimes too many any things are out of our control. Maybe that is the universe's way of making us slow down and concentrate on what really matters in life.

In my experience, my relationships come first and foremost. My family and friends and the people in my life are number one. Relationships are what make me want to be a better person in this world. No matter what the level of the relationships is, I try my best.

I was taught to never give up on my dreams, that life is too short for that. I have this dream of seeing more humanity in the world. Humanity is what is needed. More love and acceptance of others, not hate. If love was more predominating in this world, wouldn't Earth be a better place?

On that note, I will leave you with a list of thirty things that I have learned as I have aged that have helped me find my way when life changed my plans:

1. Don't let negativity eat you up and don't take on other people's issues.

2. Be honest and truthful. (That doesn't mean hurt someone's feelings.)

3. Think before you speak. Filter your thoughts through your heart to make sure your words are compassionate.

4. Don't limit yourself when it comes to friends. And ask yourself, *Are my friends healthy for me?*

5. Use your voice. It has taken me way too long to learn that, and I suggest you start today if you haven't already.

6. Don't accept hate or intolerance—neither is ever OK.

7. Treasure the happy times in life, and they will make the sad times somewhat easier.

8. Accept yourself for who you are.

9. Don't punish yourself for eating something you love.

10. Have compassion and kindness for others.

11. Don't make assumptions about people. Remember, you never know someone's story or past unless they have shared it with you.

12. Be a kind human being.

13. Help the world. If you are upset with the way the world is heading, and then do something to spread more joy and love.

14. Do something that makes you happy every day. In fact, do something fun today! Our ridiculous to do lists will be there in the morning.

15. Think of your food as joy—remember to enjoy it!

16. Try something that challenges you. Sometimes it works out and sometimes it doesn't—that's OK.

17. Remember, you have gifts and talents to offer people. Your gifts and talents could make a difference in someone's life.

18. Hug and appreciate all your animals. I believe they are angels sent down to us.

19. Hug and appreciate the family and friends you are connected too.

20. Let people know you appreciate them. It can go a long way.

21. Don't be so quick to judge others by their looks, give them a chance. I have met the most amazing people by living my life this way.

22. Are you creating time for yourself? I'm big into alone time to recharge and face the world.

23. Have you created the peaceful home environment you have always wanted? I believe that if you feel at peace at home, then everything will work better. I treasure my essential oil diffusers, my comfy-cozy bed, and the wonderful greeting I get from my lab when I get home. We all feel ourselves fully when we are home in a safe and loving environment. My dream is for all people to have safe and loving places to call home.

24. Have an open heart and compassion for someone with mental diseases. Understand that just because someone looks fine on the outside, it doesn't mean that they do not have a mental condition. Mental disease is something that sometimes can't be seen.

25. Treat people with respect. By now, you know I have strong issues with that. Because I can't stand when people don't treat me with respect. It's not OK. It's never OK to look down on someone.

26. Never take people for granted. You will regret that one day when they are longer there.

27. Remember to tell your spouse or partner, you love them.

28. Friends come in all ages, don't limit you. Some of my closest friends are older and I appreciate their wisdom and expertise.

29. Don't let one person's negative opinion stop you from living your dreams.

30. Let go of the idea that life might not always end up the way that you want it too. Go on the ride of life and see what unfolds. You can find your way, even if life changes your plans.

For reading this book all the way to the end, I thank you from the bottom of my heart. You have helped me fulfill my heart's intention to make sure that all the people who saved my life in the beginning know that the life they worked so hard to save has not been wasted.

From this day forward, I will continue to live a life of service. To do my best to make a difference in this huge world. To honor the woman who died giving birth to me. To pay tribute to my parents by being the best human being I can be, and not letting their life lessons be wasted on me. To fight for what I believe in. To use my voice that I have struggled so long to find. To live every day to the fullest, and hope that I help someone find their way along their life path.

Pain always holds a lesson, even if it is to help turn us around by looking at the positive side. If all the pain and grief that I have expressed in this book will help others out there, I know it will have been worth it. For you who have seen your struggles reflected in mine, you are not alone. You have a friend in the universe who understands you with compassion and love.

V. Lakshmi

Acknowledgments

Who I Am

I am who I am because of the people in my life, grateful to all of my family and friends — the people who are still here and the people who have passed.

The lessons they have bestowed on me are the reasons why I live my life the way I do.

Their honesty, their compassion and the knowledge that they have passed down to me always runs through my soul.

Not a lesson was wasted... and never will be on what type of human being to be.

I am always watching and learning from them through my youthful eyes... my adult eyes... observing all the examples of how to be a good human being.

I hold on to them and if I achieve anything even remotely close to what I was taught from others...

I will feel that I would have honored them in a way they so deserve to be honored:

To give back to this world, and to not take.

To leave a footprint of positivity.

The joy and the tears, Life's precious moments

Walking through them... never alone.

The friendships and family that have held me up when I have fallen down, their hand out reached to me, whenever I needed it... forever grateful I am to them.

Always there for me when I needed them to be — in life, that matters.

To be loved unconditionally.

To have no judgments or criticisms passed my way.

To be accepted for the real I and not what people want me to be.

To feel safe and loved.

To be heard and valued is what they all have given me.

The respect that I have bestowed upon them... was given back to me.

Now as an adult and a role model to younger family members, I still learn so much from them.

As I have aged I realized how important it is to be a role model to them, those special children in my life that mean the world to me.

May I be the person who they need me to be.

May I honor those before me.

May I live a legacy that would make my family and friends proud of me.

To all of you, thank you so much.

I am me, because of all of you.

I love you all.

About the Author

V. LAKSHMI, author of *Finding Your Way When Life Changes Your Plans* and international award-winning photographer, owned and ran a photography business in the Midwestern United States for eight years, before becoming a full-time writer. Looking through the lens of her camera, she developed a unique perspective for dealing with the myriad boulders life has thrown her way, and now weaves her vision into words.

V.'s uncommon life story began when was born an orphan in a remote village in India who was later adopted and raised by a white Jewish family in America. An eternal optimist, she holds a Bachelors of General Studies with Minors in Psychology and Gender Studies and keeps one goal in her heart: that her stories inspire and help out as many people as she can before she leaves this planet.

To contact her, visit www.VLakshmiAuthor.com.

How to Donate to the Family Village Farm

One of my favorite quotes is Mahatma Gandhi's *"You must be the change you wish to see in the world."* If you are looking for a wonderful way to make a difference, and you want enrich a child's life, please think about donating. —V. Lakshmi

To learn more about Family Village Farm and its founder, visit:

www.globalministries.org/child_sponsorship
www.globalministries.org/pauline_king_corner#letter
www.globalministries.org/pauline_king_corner

Publisher's Note: How to Help Spread the Word

If you enjoyed this book, kindly support the author by helping others find it. Here are suggestions to consider:

- Write an online customer review wherever books are sold

- Gift this book to those who will benefit from its messages

- Share a book photo on social media and tag #VLakshmi

- Bring in V. Lakshmi as a speaker for your organization

- Suggest *Finding Your Way* to your local book club

- Call Citrine Publishing at (828) 585-7030 for large orders